# 108 VEGAN RECIPES
(Grain/Gluten-Free)

**Other Publications by Touchstone Media:**

*Bhaktivinoda Vāṇī Vaibhava*
*Prārthanā*
*Śrī Prema Bhakti-candrikā*
*Sārvabhauma Śataka*
*Hari Bhakti Kalpa Latika*
*Śrī Nityānanda-caritāmṛta*
*Pada Sevana*
*Sweet Pastimes of Damodara*
*The Dog and the Wolf*
*Great Heroes of the Mahābhārata Series*
*Krishna Pocket Guide*
*Amṛta Vāṇī*
*Śrī Prema Vilāsa*
*Uddhava Gītā*
*Adventures of India Series*
*Śrī Krishna Vijaya*
*Mahābhārata*
*Bhagavad-gītā at a Glance*
*Vrindāvana, the Playground of God*
*Govardhana, the Hill that Fulfills all Desires*
*Patrāmṛta*
*Heart and Soul Connection*
*Śrīmati's Vegetarian Delight*
*Gita Stories from Padma Purana*
*Vaktṛtavalī*
*Sri Ksetra, Vaikuntha on Earth*
*Tales of Devotion Series*

If you are interested in the purchasing or the distribution of this book or any of the above publications, you may contact:

Touchstone Media
Vrindavan 281121, INDIA
www.touchstonemedia.com
e-mail : sales@touchstonemedia.com

# 108 VEGAN RECIPES

## (Grain/Gluten-Free)

Krishna Priya Dasi

Edited by MadanMohanMohini Dasi

TOUCHSTONE MEDIA

*Matter for the Soul*

108 Vegan Recipes
Krishna Priya Dasi
Edited by MadanMohanMohini Dasi
Produced and Published by Īśvara Dāsa
Book Layout and Cover Design by Harihara Dāsa
Photography by Bhaktin Cheryl Elia, Ananda-lila Dāsī, and Sundari-radha Dāsī
Printed at M/s Royal Press, New Delhi, INDIA

ISBN: 978-81-957907-3-9

HARE KṚṢṆA HARE KṚṢṆA
KṚṢṆA KṚṢṆA HARE HARE
HARE RAMA HARE RAMA
RAMA RAMA HARE HARE

**1. Sravanam** (Hearing)

Radha's absorbed in the transcendental sound
And experiences supreme spiritual pleasure.
She is effulgent with endless ecstasy
And feels fortunate beyond measure.

His Divine Grace A.C. Bhaktivedanta Swami Prabhupada
Founder Acharya of the International Society
for Krishna Consciousness (ISKCON)

All glories to His Divine Grace Srila Prabhupada,
Who is the source of all our inspiration.
He's taught us to cook for Kṛṣṇa joyfully
With purity and complete dedication.

# Content

**2. Kirtanam** (Chanting)
I sing Your glories, names, pastimes,
Which are like the rays of the full moon.
They increase the ocean of divine bliss
Like the blackish clouds of the monsoon.

# Acknowledgment

I cannot express my deep gratitude to my mother Srimati Maina Devi Jeendgar, for teaching me the art of cooking and to my father Shri Shyam Lal Jeendgar for always encouraging and appreciating my cooking.

I am eternally indebted to my spiritual master, His Holiness Lokanath Swami, for accepting me as his disciple and always giving me his blessings, guidance, and encouragement in my devotional services.

I am very grateful to my husband, Gopal Das, for always supporting my devotional projects.

I am very thankful to my sisters, Sunita Agarwal and Vandana Agarwal, my brother Pawan Jeendgar, and my mother-in-law Nancie Rosenberg for always encouraging me and helping me to engage in devotional services.

One of the greatest blessings is from Lord Krsna - my connection with Her Grace MadanMohanMohini Dasi, who has been editing my books with complete dedication and talent for years.

My deepest gratitude goes to His Grace Isvara Das from the touchstone publishing company for dedicating his valuable time to publishing this cookbook.

I am very grateful to Priya Ghatwai for testing the dishes from this cookbook.

I am so impressed with the photos of the dishes for this cookbook taken by Bhaktin Cheryl Elia, Ananda Lila Dasi, and Sundari Radha Dasi. My special thanks to them.

My deepest gratitude goes to His Grace Harihara Das for dedicating his full attention, time, and talent to lay out this cookbook.

Above all, tremendous gratitude goes to the Supreme Personality of Godhead, Lord Kṛṣṇa, for His mercy in engaging me in different services to serve Srila Prabhupada's transcendental movement, ISKCON, the International Society for Krsna Consciousness.

**3. Smaranam** (Remembering)
Radha meditates on Kṛṣṇa;
He is Her life and soul.
Being absorbed in transcendental thoughts
She reaches Her desired goal.

# 108 Vegan Recipes

(GRAIN/GLUTEN-FREE)

His Divine Grace A. C. Bhaktivedanta Swami Prabhupada, the Founder-Acharya of the International Society for Krishna Consciousness (ISKCON) expertly engaged everyone in devotional service to Lord Kṛṣṇa according to their psycho-physical natures, whether they print and distribute transcendental literature, cook, sing, write, etc.

Any activity will become blissful and have eternal value if done for the Supreme Person, Kṛṣṇa.

We understand that the Supreme Lord Krsna loves cows and He prioritizes their protection and happiness above all others. Unfortunately, in most places in the world today, it has become very difficult to get pure cow's milk and there is no guarantee that today's cow's milk is not mixed with other animals' milk. Also, the milk is often over-pasteurized and homogenized, and different hormones are given to cows to increase their milk production. Because of these things, many people have developed problems with their health, so their doctors recommend avoiding milk products altogether. Also, many soft-hearted, compassionate people will object to the abominable and exploitative way cows are mistreated in the dairy industry. So, although eating of those bountiful gifts that our dear mother cow may otherwise be a loving reciprocation with her, that sweet exchange is hardly possible in today's world. In light of this, my husband and I were inspired to give an opportunity for all those that have these legitimate concerns to still enjoy wonderful prasadam dishes without compromising their physical health or personal ethical convictions. This vegan cookbook is also grain and gluten-free because many people follow this diet.

Thank you very much. Hare Kṛṣṇa.
Your servant,

Krishna Priya Dasi

Krishna Priya Dasi

**4. Pada Sevanam** (Serving the Feet)
My life's only meaning and treasure
Is to serve Your lotus feet.
They are just like lotus flowers:
Soft, sublime, and sweet.

# Author's Note

We are all seeking happiness and are often looking for a companion to experience that happiness. Proper relationships provide a sense of meaning and purpose in life and help us gain the confidence to attain our desired goals. But where to find such a person when we often experience selfishness and uncertainty in our relationships? Is there someone who can introduce us to that companion who will always be with us no matter what the situation? Someone who will walk with us until we reach our destination? Yes, there is such a special person: His Divine Grace A.C. Bhaktivedanta Swami Prabhupada, the Founder-Acharya of the International Society for Krishna Consciousness (ISKCON). It is his transcendental literature that will actually introduce us to that companion.

There are so many writings – fiction, histories, and so on – but none can solve life's problems. Srila Prabhupada translated more than sixty volumes of Vedic literature from the original Sanskrit text into English, which gives the sacred understanding and conclusion of all knowledge. Though the matters discussed are philosophical, his devotional and scholarly commentaries are easy to apply in our daily lives and will completely satisfy the questioning mind. We can attain eternal happiness by studying transcendental literature such as Bhagavad-gita As It Is, Srimad Bhagavatam, and Sri Caitanya-caritamrta, etc.

It doesn't matter which of his books you choose to read; by absorbing your mind in them, you can completely deal with and resolve all the worries and pressures of everyday life. At the same time, you will be able to explore the author's philosophical and magnanimous explanations. The wisdom from these Vedic literatures is timeless; in other words, it applies to all persons at all times. Although this information was initially transmitted through aural reception five thousand years ago, it was written down by Srila Vyasadeva and is today passed down to us through an unbroken chain of spiritual preceptors called the parampara.

So whether you are looking for solutions to cultural, scientific, global, or personal dilemmas, you can read the writings of His Divine Grace A.C. Bhaktivedanta Swami Prabhupada and find all the answers. I therefore wholeheartedly request you to do an experiment and begin reading these beautiful literatures and see how things change – for the better – in your life. This companionship will bestow inner peace upon your life and will take you to that place of eternal bliss and knowledge.

Srila Prabhupada's books can be purchased from all ISKCON centers and online.

Thank you very much. Hare Kṛṣṇa.
Your servant,

Krishna Priya Dasi

**5. Arcanam** (Offering Worship)
I worship you with Vṛndāvana flowers
And offer My heart and devotion.
You wear the fragrance of divine love
And You're the focus of My adoration.

**6. Vandanam** (Offering Prayers)
You are the only object of My prayers
From dawn to dusk and dusk to dawn.
O ocean of causeless mercy and bliss
Kindly consider Me as Your own.

# Words Of Encouragement

How many of us have asked ourselves why we suffer and how to stop our suffering? Do we wonder how we got here and where we're going at the end of this life, or do we think that there's nothing more after this life? Do we have more questions that still need to be answered? And are there answers to these questions?

We have so many questions. Even the birds and beasts ask questions – in different languages – but their questions are focused only on how to eat, sleep, mate, and defend. The consciousness of human beings, however, is more developed so that we can ask more elevated questions such as the ones above. And yes, there are answers.

You may be asking what all of this has to do with a cookbook. Well, this is not an ordinary cookbook because it is written as an offering to the Supreme Lord, Sri Kṛṣṇa. In this cookbook, you will learn not only the art of preparing delicious foodstuffs but also the path of inner peace and happiness by connecting with the right literature and sound vibration. You will also learn the importance of offering these preparations to the Lord and then will be able to partake in sanctified food. Understanding these spiritual topics and the answers to the above inquiries takes purification of the heart and elevation of consciousness. And that's where the "Words of Encouragement" come in.

If I suggest that by chanting a mantra – meaning to free the mind from anxiety and the material concept of life – you would be transported from suffering to an eternally blissful life and realize who you are, would you believe me? Well, it is not only genuinely believable but truly attainable!

Five hundred years ago in West Bengal, India, Sri Caitanya Mahaprabhu, who is Lord Kṛṣṇa Himself, appeared to teach the chanting of this mantra:

Hare Kṛṣṇa Hare Kṛṣṇa
Kṛṣṇa Kṛṣṇa Hare Hare
Hare Rama Hare Rama
Rama Rama Hare Hare

This transcendental sound vibration elevates our consciousness from the mundane to the spiritual platform and is recommended in this age to solve all problems. It's full of mercy, compassion, fulfillment, and love and is the rarest treasure in the world.

Srila Prabhupada gives a wonderful expanded translation (Cc Madhya-lila 17.133)

"The holy name of Kṛṣṇa is transcendentally blissful. It bestows all spiritual benedictions, for it is Himself Kṛṣṇa, the reservoir of all pleasure. Kṛṣṇa's name is complete, and it is the form of all transcendental mellows. It is not a material name under any condition, and it is no less powerful than Kṛṣṇa Himself. Since Kṛṣṇa's name is not contaminated by the material qualities, there is no question of its being involved with maya. Kṛṣṇa's name is always liberated and spiritual. It is never conditioned by the laws of material nature. This is because Kṛṣṇa's name and Kṛṣṇa Himself are identical."

So considering all that has been said, please try to chant this wonderful Hare Kṛṣṇa mantra and experience happiness yourself. You will find that all the answers to life's questions will be revealed and the only thing you'll lose are misery and anxiety! And from chanting Hare Kṛṣṇa, you will begin to understand why this mantra is so special.

There is so much more to be said about chanting Hare Kṛṣṇa. For further information on this divine mantra, you can read Srila Prabhupada's books or contact any ISKCON center.

MadanMohanMohini Dasi

**7. Dasyam** (Servant)
Devotional service to My Lord Kṛṣṇa
Is sublime and very sweet.
When completely absorbed in service
I feel that My life's complete.

# A Devotional Offering

Lord Kṛṣṇa states in the *Bhagavad-gita 9.26*:

patram puspam phalam toyam
yo me bhaktya prayacchati
tad aham bhakty-upahrtam
asnami prayatatmanah

"If one offers Me with love and devotion a leaf, a flower, a fruit or water, I will accept it."
It is said that the way to a man's heart is through his stomach. Yes, food is one way we can show affection and care for someone. If food is cooked to please Lord Kṛṣṇa, the Supreme Person, the enjoyer, and reservoir of pleasure, then our cooking attains perfection. The real purpose of preparing and offering food to Lord Kṛṣṇa is to express our love and devotion to Him. Although Lord Kṛṣṇa is complete in Himself and does not need anything, he allows us to cook and offer food to Him out of His unlimited kindness.

Srila Prabhupada gives an excellent expanded translation in (Bhagavad-gita 9.26)

One who loves Kṛṣṇa will give Him whatever He wants, and he avoids offering anything which is undesirable or unasked. Thus meat, fish, and eggs should not be offered to Kṛṣṇa. If He desired such things as offerings, He would have said so. Instead, He clearly requests that a leaf, fruit, flowers, and water be given to Him, and He says of this offering, "I will accept it." Therefore, we should understand that He will not accept meat, fish, and eggs.

When we cook for Lord Kṛṣṇa, cleanliness is very important, so we must first wash our hands. While cooking, we do not taste the food; the meal is meant for Lord Kṛṣṇa to enjoy first, so He should taste it first. It's best for the offering to have a new set of dinnerware to be used only for Lord Kṛṣṇa and not to be used by anyone else. If we are offering to Visnu-tattva

(Lord Kṛṣṇa and Lord Caitanya, etc.), and we understand the importance of Tulasi and have a Tulasi plant, we should put a Tulasi leaf on each preparation.

We may offer to Kṛṣṇa or God as we know Him by preparing an altar in a clean place in our home. If possible, we should make a curtain that can be closed when we make an offering and while Lord Kṛṣṇa eats. We can place three pictures on the altar: as we're facing the altar, on the left, there should be a picture of Srila Prabhupada, the spiritual master and Founder-Acharya (teacher) of the International Society for Krishna Consciousness (If initiated by someone other than Srila Prabhupada, we would place the picture of our spiritual master to the left of Srila Prabhupada's, and if not yet initiated, we would have Srila Prabhupada's picture). The picture of the Panca Tattva would be in the middle, and Sri Sri Radha-Kṛṣṇa's photo would be on the right side. We may say the following prayers, chant the Hare Kṛṣṇa mantra, or humbly ask the Lord to accept our offering. If we chant these prayers, each of the following mantras should be recited three times while ringing a small bell. The most important aspect of cooking and offering our food is our love and devotion.

Prayer to Srila Prabhupada:

nama om vishnu-padaya Kṛṣṇa-presthaya bhutale
srimate bhaktivedanta-svamin iti namine namas te
sarasvate deve gaura-vani-pracharine
nirvishesha-shunyavadi-paschatya-desha tarine

"I offer my respectful obeisances unto His Divine Grace A.C. Bhaktivedanta Swami Prabhupada, who is very dear to Lord Kṛṣṇa, having taken shelter at His lotus feet. Our respectful obeisances unto you, O spiritual master, servant of Sarasvati Goswami. You are kindly preaching the message of Lord Chaitanya and delivering the Western countries, which are filled with impersonalism and voidism."

Prayer to Lord Caitanya:
namo maha-vadanyaya Kṛṣṇa-prema-pradaya te
Kṛṣṇaya Kṛṣṇa-chaitanya-namne gaura-tvishe namaha

“I offer my respectful obeisances unto the Supreme Lord Sri Kṛṣṇa Caitanya, who is more magnanimous than any other incarnation, even Kṛṣṇa Himself because He is bestowing freely what no one else has ever given - pure love of Kṛṣṇa.

Prayer to Lord Kṛṣṇa:

namo-brahmanya-devaya go brahmana hitaya cha
jagad-hitaya Kṛṣṇaya govindaya namo namaha

“I offer my respectful obeisances to the Supreme Absolute Truth, Kṛṣṇa, who is the well-wisher of the cows and the Brahmanas as well as the living entities in general. I offer my repeated obeisances to Govinda [Kṛṣṇa], who is the pleasure reservoir for all the senses.”

If you like, you can also chant the following mantra, called the maha-mantra, or great mantra, several times:

Hare Kṛṣṇa Hare Kṛṣṇa
Kṛṣṇa Kṛṣṇa Hare Hare
Hare Rama Hare Rama
Rama Rama Hare Hare

After offering the food to the Lord, wait for at least 10-15 minutes for Him to partake in the preparations. After removing the offering from the altar, we should transfer the food from Lord Kṛṣṇa’s dinnerware either into the original pots or onto a clean plate or transfer container and then wash and dry the plates, bowls, etc. Everything that we offered with love and devotion is now prasada, the mercy of the Lord. When we offer the Lord something with pure consciousness, the remnants become non-different from Him. So we should not only honor prasada with great respect, but we should distribute it to others as well. This is the perfection of cooking.

MadanMohanMohini Dasi

**8. Sakhyam** (Friendship)
I place My hands in Your Hands,
O My supreme and eternal friend.
Being with You is most pleasurable,
And I hope this will never end.

# Festive Invitation

A little over 500 years ago, Sri Caitanya Mahaprabhu appeared in West Bengal, India. His mission was to spread the chanting of the Lord's holy names – Hare Kṛṣṇa , Hare Kṛṣṇa , Kṛṣṇa  Kṛṣṇa , Hare Hare/ Hare Rama, Hare Rama, Rama Rama, Hare Hare - to every town and village across the globe. Together with His followers, they would blissfully sing and dance to traditional instruments' accompaniment, introducing everyone to the holy names. Thus the Hare Kṛṣṇa  movement was started.

Lord Caitanya personally traveled all over India, bringing joy and peace to all who met or saw Him. His compassion for all living entities, whether human beings, animals, those in the plant kingdom, etc., set the example of how kindness and respect should be given to every living being.

During His travels, many festivals were held where sumptuous prasada or sanctified, pure vegetarian foodstuffs were distributed to everyone, which brought even more bliss to those present. To this day, Lord Caitanya's followers continue this motto of chanting, dancing, and feasting by inviting everyone to come to their nearby Hare Kṛṣṇa temple, especially on Sundays when they hold their traditional Sunday feast. Therefore, we invite you to go to your nearest Hare Kṛṣṇa  temple and partake in this feast and other festivals held throughout the year. There are also Hare Kṛṣṇa  restaurants, many named "Govinda's," where you can enjoy delicious foodstuffs every day of the year.

MadanMohanMohini Dasi

**9. Atma Nivedanam** (Surrendering Everything)
I fully surrender Myself to You,
O creator, maintainer, enjoyer forever.
You're the fountain of unconditional love
And in You, I will always take full shelter.

# Notes

1. It is better to start with a little water and gradually add more to obtain the batter's and dough's proper consistency. You can also adjust the quantity of water needed for cooking.
2. In this cookbook, sunflower oil is used, but you may use the oil of your choice.
3. The time given for cooking, frying, or baking is approximate. The amount of time will differ according to the type of stove, pot, and oven you use; cooking takes less time on a gas stove (as opposed to an electric stove). The thickness of the bottom of your pot and how quickly you stir the preparation will also determine how everything cooks. Therefore, you will need to check to ensure your preparation is ready to take to the next step.
4. Powdered sugar generally contains cornstarch, which is often considered a grain; I usually grind sugar in a spice grinder or a blender to make my powdered sugar. I use white sugar in my recipes as it is most often used in India, but you can use turbinado, organic cane sugar, or raw sugar instead. The flavors and sweetness vary slightly.
5. Some ingredients need to be ground in a food processor rather than a blender; you will need to use what is specifically written in the recipe.
6. When using leafy vegetables such as spinach, cilantro, etc, firmly pack them into the measuring cup or spoon.
7. I am not stating the boiling time for vegetables like potatoes, plantains, taro root, pumpkin, etc., because the time varies according to how it is done, whether you use a pressure cooker or saucepan.
8. In several recipes, I use asafetida to enhance the flavor of the preparation; however, it is optional.
9. Preparation and cooking time will vary from person to person.
10. You Can adjust the amount of salt, spices, sugar, and oil accordingly.
11. Green chilies are used a lot in Indian cooking; however, you can reduce the amount of chilies according to your taste or you can completely avoid using them altogether according to your taste.

# Key Measurements

I use a teaspoon, tablespoon, and cup to measure the ingredients as well as ml to measure liquid ingredients. I am only using the American cup and spoon measurements.

TEASPOON
The American, Australian, and British teaspoons all hold approximately 5 ml.

TABLESPOON
The American tablespoon holds 14.2 ml, the Australian tablespoon holds 20 ml, and the British tablespoon holds 17.7 ml.

CUP
The American and British cups hold 240 ml, and the Australian cup holds 250 ml.

TEMPERATURE
The temperature for deep-frying and the oven is given first in Fahrenheit then in Celsius. A cooking thermometer is required to measure the temperature of the oil.

# Soups and Saladas

# Salads and Soups

# Swami Soup

These recipes have a secret ingredient: the blessings and encouragement from my spiritual master, His Holiness Lokanath Swami. Having the shelter of a bona fide spiritual master is certainly the greatest fortune and success in human life.

Preparation and cooking time
**35 Min.**

Serves
**2-3 Persons**

## Ingredients

- 2 cups broccoli florets
- 2 cups cauliflower florets
- ¼ cup pumpkin seeds
- 1 tablespoon ginger, peeled and roughly chopped
- 4 cups (960 ml) water
- 1½ teaspoons oil
- ½ teaspoon cumin seeds
- 1 teaspoon salt
- ¼ teaspoon black pepper

## Procedure

1. Combine the broccoli, cauliflower, pumpkin seeds, ginger, and water in a 6-quart stockpot. Cover and boil the vegetables over medium-high heat for 15-20 minutes or until they become tender. Uncover the pot and stir a few times with a wooden spatula to make sure the vegetables do not stick and are evenly cooked. Allow to cool, then blend in a blender until a smooth puree.

2. Heat the oil in a 3-quart saucepan over medium heat. When it is hot but not smoking, add the cumin seeds and sauté until light brown. Add the puree, salt, and black pepper. Cook for 3-4 minutes. If needed, you can add extra water.

# Priya Soup

Srimati Radharani has many names, one of which is Priya, which means dear. She gives Lord Kṛṣṇa the most pleasure from Her incomparable devotional service and is, therefore, the most dear to Him. She is His pleasure potency and loves to cook for Him and received the blessing from Durvasa Muni that She would be able to cook a new preparation every day for Lord Kṛṣṇa's pleasure.

Cashew pieces soaking time **12-15 Min.**

Preparation and cooking time **35 Min.**

Serves **3-4 Persons**

## Ingredients

- ¾ cup cashew pieces
- 1 cup coconut milk
- 1 tablespoon oil
- ¼ teaspoon asafetida
- 1½ cups celery, cut into small pieces
- 1½ cups pumpkin, peeled, seeded, and cut into small pieces
- 1½ cups (360 ml) water, or as needed
- 2 cups kale
- 2 cups spinach
- ¾ teaspoon salt
- ¼ teaspoon black pepper
- 1½ teaspoons cumin powder

## Procedure

1. Soak the cashew pieces in the coconut milk for 12-15 minutes. Transfer to a blender and process until a smooth paste. Transfer to a bowl. Set aside.

2. Heat the oil in a 6-quart stockpot over medium heat. Add the asafetida. Continuously stirring, cook for a few seconds. Add the celery, pumpkin, and water. Cover the pot and cook for 4-5 minutes.

3. Add the kale and spinach. Cook for 8-10 minutes or until all the vegetables are cooked. Allow to cool. Transfer to a blender and process until a smooth puree.

4. Transfer to the pot. Add the cashew and coconut milk paste, salt, pepper, and cumin powder. Heat for 3-4 minutes. You can add extra hot water if needed.

Priya Soup

# Butternut Squash And Quinoa Soup

Quinoa is one of the healthiest foods and becoming increasingly popular. I have added several quinoa recipes for healthy eating.

Preparation and cooking time
**35 Min.**

Serves
**2-3 Persons**

## Ingredients

- 1 tablespoon oil
- 1 teaspoon cumin powder
- 1 tablespoon ginger root, peeled and finely chopped
- ¾ tablespoon green chilies, finely chopped
- 2 cups tomatoes, finely chopped
- 2 cups butternut squash, peeled and cut into 1-inch (2.5 cm) pieces
- ¾ teaspoon salt
- ⅛ teaspoon black pepper
- 2 cups (480 ml) water, or as needed
- 1 cup cooked quinoa

## Procedure

1. Heat the oil in a 3-quart saucepan over medium heat. When it is hot but not smoking, add the cumin seeds and sauté until they turn brown. Add the ginger root and green chilies. Continuously stirring, cook for a few seconds.

2. Add the tomatoes. Occasionally stirring, cook for 4-5 minutes. Add the butternut squash, salt, black pepper, and water. Cover the pan and cook for 15-20 minutes or until the butternut squash becomes tender. Uncover the pan and stir a few times with a wooden spatula while cooking to make sure the vegetables are evenly cooked and do not stick. Add the quinoa. You can add extra water if needed.

NOTE: You can add 3 tablespoons of chopped peanuts or cashews to the soup for a nice nutty taste.

# Sweet Potato And Tomato Soup

Preparation and cooking time
**30 Min.**

Serves
**3-4 Persons**

## Ingredients

- 1½ cups sweet potatoes, peeled and cut into medium-sized pieces
- 3 cups tomatoes, cut into medium- sized pieces
- 2 cups (480 ml) water, or as needed
- 1 teaspoon oil
- ¼ teaspoon asafetida
- 2 cups kale, finely chopped
- ¼ teaspoon salt
- pinch of black pepper

## Procedure

1. Combine the potatoes, tomatoes, and water in a 3-quart saucepan. Cover and boil the vegetables over medium-high heat for 15-20 minutes or until they become tender. Allow to cool, then blend in a blender until a smooth puree.

2. Heat the oil in a 3-quart saucepan. Add the asafetida. Continuously stirring, cook for a few seconds. Add the chopped kale and continuously stirring, cook for 2-3 minutes. Add the salt, black pepper, and puree. Cook for 3-4 minutes. If needed, you can add extra water.

# Mixed Vegetable Soup

Preparation and cooking time
**25 Min.**

Serves
**3-4 Persons**

## Ingredients

- 2 cups tomatoes, cut into medium-sized pieces
- 2 cups broccoli florets
- 3 cups kale
- 1½ tablespoons ginger root peeled and roughly chopped
- 2 cups (480 ml) water, or as needed
- ¾ teaspoon salt
- pinch of black pepper
- ½ cup cabbage, finely shredded
- ½ cup carrots, peeled and grated

## Procedure

1. Combine the tomatoes, broccoli, kale, ginger root, and water in a 6-quart stockpot. Cover the pot and cook over medium-high heat for 12-15 minutes or until the vegetables become tender.

2. Uncover the pot and stir a few times with a wooden spatula while cooking to make sure the vegetables do not stick and are evenly cooked. Allow to cool. Blend in a blender until smooth puree. Transfer to a 6-quart stockpot.

3. Add the salt, black pepper, cabbage, and carrots. Cook for 2-3 minutes; the cabbage and carrots should be crunchy. If needed, you can add extra water.

# Broccoli And Spinach Soup

Preparation and cooking time
**30 Min.**

Serves
**3-4 Persons**

## Ingredients

- 3 cups broccoli florets
- 2 cups spinach
- 3 cups (720 ml) water, or as needed
- 1½ cups coconut milk
- 1 tablespoon ginger root, peeled and roughly chopped
- ½ teaspoon salt
- ⅛ teaspoon black pepper

## Procedure

1. Combine the broccoli florets, spinach, water, coconut milk, and ginger root in a 6-quart stockpot. Cover the pot and cook over medium heat for 15-20 minutes or until the vegetables become tender.

2. Uncover the pot and stir a few times with a wooden spatula while cooking to make sure the vegetables do not stick and are evenly cooked. Transfer to a bowl. Allow to cool. Blend in a blender until smooth puree.

3. Transfer to a 6-quart stockpot. Add the salt and black pepper. Cook for 2-3 minutes.

# Creamy Spinach Soup

Preparation and cooking time
**20 Min.**

Serves
**2-3 Persons**

## Ingredients

- ½ lb. (226 grams) spinach
- ¾ cup cashew pieces
- 1 tablespoon ginger root, peeled and roughly chopped
- ½ teaspoon salt
- ¼ teaspoon paprika
- ¼ teaspoon black pepper
- 1 teaspoon sugar
- 2 cups (480 ml) water, or as needed

## Procedure

1. Place all the ingredients in a 3-quart saucepan. Cook uncovered over medium-high heat for 8-10 minutes or until the spinach becomes soft.

2. Allow to cool, then blend in a blender until a smooth puree. Warm the soup before serving.

# Quinoa And Vegetable Soup

Preparation and cooking time
**40 Min.**

Serves
**3-4 Persons**

## Ingredients

- 2½ cups (600 ml) water, or as needed
- 2 cups coconut milk
- 1 cup broccoli, cut into ¾-inch (2 cm) florets
- 1 cup celery, cut into ¾-inch (2 cm) pieces
- 1 cup bell pepper, cut into ¾-inch (2 cm) pieces
- 1 cup zucchini, cut into ¾-inch (2 cm) pieces
- 1 tablespoon ginger root, peeled and grated
- ½ cup quinoa
- 1 teaspoon salt
- ¼ black pepper
- 1 teaspoon cumin powder

## Procedure

1. Place the water and coconut milk in a 6-quart stockpot. Cook over medium-high heat.

2. Add all the remaining ingredients. Cover the pot and cook over medium heat for 20-22 minutes or until the vegetables and quinoa are cooked. Stir the vegetables and quinoa a few times with a wooden spatula to make sure the vegetables do not stick and are evenly cooked. You can add extra water if the soup becomes too thick.

# Celery And Zucchini Soup

Preparation and cooking time
**40 Min.**

Serves
**2-3 Persons**

## Ingredients

- 2 tablespoons oil
- ⅓ cup almonds, ground
- 2 cups celery, cut into 1-inch (2.5 cm) pieces
- 2 cups zucchini, cut into 1-inch (2.5 cm) pieces
- 1½ tablespoons ginger root peeled and roughly chopped
- 4 cups (960 ml) water, or as needed
- ¾ teaspoon salt
- ⅛ teaspoon black pepper
- ½ teaspoon dried oregano

## Procedure

1. Heat the oil in a 6-quart stockpot. Add the almonds. Continuously stirring, cook over medium heat for 30 seconds -1 minute or until they become light brown. Add the celery, zucchini, ginger root, and water.

2. Cover the pot and cook over medium-high heat for 20-25 minutes or until the vegetables are cooked. Stir a few times with a wooden spatula while cooking to make sure the vegetables do not stick and are evenly cooked.

3. Allow to cool. Blend in a blender until smooth puree.

4. Transfer to a 6-quart stockpot. Add the salt, black pepper, and oregano. Warm for a few minutes over medium heat. If needed, you can add extra water.

# Peanut And Vegetable Soup

Preparation and cooking time
**35 Min.**

Serves
**2-3 Persons**

## Ingredients

- 2 cups pumpkin, peeled, seeded, and cut into medium-sized pieces
- 1 cup potatoes, peeled and cut into medium-sized pieces
- 1 cup yellow bell peppers, cut into medium-sized pieces
- 2 tablespoons peanut butter
- 3 cups (720 ml) water, or as needed
- ¾ teaspoon salt
- ⅛ teaspoon black pepper
- ¼ cup blanched peanuts, roasted and crushed

## Procedure

1. Combine the pumpkin, potatoes, bell peppers, peanut butter, and water in a 6-quart stockpot. Cover the pot and cook over medium-high heat for 15-20 minutes or until the vegetables are cooked. Stir a few times with a wooden spatula while cooking to make sure they do not stick and are evenly cooked.

2. Allow to cool. Blend in a blender until smooth puree.

3. Transfer to a 6-quart stockpot. Add the salt, black pepper, and peanuts. Warm for a few minutes over medium heat.

NOTE: Blending the vegetables is optional.

# Green Soup With Baked Sweet Potatoes

Baking time
**15-20 Min.**

Preparation and cooking time
**30 Min.**

Serves
**3-4 Persons**

## Ingredients

- 1 cup sweet potatoes, peeled and finely chopped
- ½ tablespoon oil
- 4 cups spinach
- 1 cup broccoli florets
- 1 cup cabbage, roughly chopped
- ⅓ cup sunflower seeds
- 1 tablespoon ginger, peeled and roughly chopped
- 1 teaspoon salt
- ⅓ teaspoon black pepper
- 1 teaspoon cumin powder
- 4 cups (960 ml) water

## Procedure

1. Combine the potatoes and oil in a bowl. Mix well. Place the potatoes in a greased 9 x 13-inch (22.5 x 32.5 cm) baking tray. Bake the potatoes in a preheated oven at 350°F (177°C) for 15-20 minutes or until they are baked. Allow to cool.

2. Place the remaining ingredients in a 6-quart stockpot. Partially cover the pot and cook over medium heat for 15-20 minutes or until the vegetables are tender. Allow to cool. Transfer to a blender. Blend until a smooth puree.

3. Transfer to a 3-quart saucepan. Cook for 3-4 minutes. Add baked potatoes. Mix well.

# Baked Vegetable Soup

Baking time
**25-30 Min.**

Preparation and cooking time
**10 Min.**

Serves
**4-5 Persons**

## Ingredients

- 3 cups cauliflower florets
- 2 cups sweet potatoes, peeled and cut into medium-sized pieces
- ½ tablespoon ginger root peeled and roughly chopped
- 6 cups (1440 ml) water, or as needed
- 1¼ teaspoons salt
- ⅛ teaspoon black pepper
- 1 teaspoon cumin powder

## Procedure

1. Place the cauliflower and sweet potatoes in a greased 9 x 13-inch (22.5 x 32.5 cm) baking tray.

2. Bake the vegetables in a preheated oven at 350°F (177°C) for 25-30 minutes or until they are baked. Allow to cool.

3. Transfer to a blender. Add the ginger root and water. Blend till a smooth puree.

4. Transfer to a 6-quart stockpot. Add the salt, black pepper, and cumin powder. Heat for a few minutes.

# Gaura Potato Salad

Preparation and cooking time
**20 Min.**

Serves
**1-2 Persons**

## Ingredients

- 2 cups potatoes, boiled, peeled, and cut into ¾-inch (2 cm) pieces
- 2 tablespoons white sesame seeds, roasted
- 2 tablespoons peanuts, roasted and ground
- ⅓ teaspoon salt
- ¼ teaspoon peppercorns, freshly coarsely ground
- 1 tablespoon lemon juice
- ½ tablespoon ginger juice
- 2 tablespoons cilantro, finely chopped

## Procedure

Place all the ingredients in a bowl. Mix gently.

# Sweet Potato Salad

I am not adding the potatoes' boiling time as it can vary according to what you use (a pressure cooker or a saucepan). Also, there are different colors of sweet potatoes; I am using white sweet potatoes for this recipe.

Preparation and cooking time
**10 Min.**

Serves
**2-3 Persons**

## Ingredients

- ⅓ cup fresh mint leaves, finely chopped
- ¾ teaspoon salt
- ¼ teaspoon black pepper
- ¼ teaspoon asafetida
- 1½ teaspoons lemon juice
- 1½ teaspoons olive oil
- 2 cups sweet potatoes, peeled, cut into 2-inch pieces and boiled

## Procedure

Combine all the ingredients in a bowl except for the potatoes. Mix well. Add the potatoes. Mix gently.

# Quinoa Salad

Preparation and cooking time
**30 Min.**

Serves
**4-5 Persons**

## Ingredients

- 1 cup quinoa
- 2 cups (480 ml) water
- 2 cups kale
- 1 cup cut bell peppers
- 1 cup cauliflower florets
- 1¼ teaspoons salt
- ¾ teaspoon paprika
- ⅓ teaspoon asafetida
- 2½ tablespoons lemon juice
- 1 tablespoon olive oil
- ½ cup carrots, peeled and shredded

## Procedure

1. Combine the quinoa and water in a 3-quart saucepan. Bring the mixture to a vigorous boil, then lower the heat and cover it. Simmer for approximately 15 minutes or until the quinoa is tender and the water has evaporated (like making rice). Transfer to a bowl to cool.

2. Combine the kale, bell peppers, and cauliflower in a food processor. Grind until smooth. Transfer to the bowl of quinoa.

3. Add the salt, paprika, asafetida, lemon juice, olive oil, and shredded carrots.

4. Mix well. Serve chilled or at room temperature.

NOTE: The vegetables can be steamed before they are ground.

# Peanut Salad

Preparation and cooking time
**35 Min.**

Serves
**3-4 Persons**

## Ingredients

- 1 cup peanuts
- 4 cups (960 ml) water
- 1½ cups broccoli slaw
- ½ cup carrots, peeled and grated
- 2 tablespoons lemon juice
- ½ teaspoon salt
- ½ teaspoon cumin powder, roasted
- ½ teaspoon peppercorns, coarsely ground

## Procedure

1. Bring the water to a boil in a 3-quart saucepan, then add the peanuts. Cover the pan and boil over medium heat for 25-30 minutes or until the peanuts are soft. You can also use a pressure cooker.

2. Strain the extra water and transfer it to a mixing bowl.

3. Add all the remaining ingredients. Mix well.

# Mixed Vegetable Salad

Preparation and cooking time
**9-10 Min.**

Serves
**1-2 Persons**

## Ingredients

- 1 teaspoon oil
- ¼ teaspoon asafetida
- ⅓ teaspoon turmeric
- 2 cups kale, finely chopped
- 1 cup cabbage, finely shredded
- 1 cup carrots, peeled and grated
- ¼ teaspoon salt
- ⅛ teaspoon cayenne pepper

## Procedure

1. Heat the oil in a frying pan over medium heat. When it is hot but not smoking, add the asafetida and turmeric and sauté for a few seconds.

2. Add the kale, cabbage, carrots, salt, and cayenne pepper. Continuously stirring, cook for 1-2 minutes.

# Kachoomar Salad

Preparation time
**20 Min.**

Serves
**2-3 Persons**

## Ingredients

- 1 cup cucumbers, peeled and cut into ½-inch (1.5 cm) pieces
- 1 cup radishes, peeled and cut into ½-inch (1.5 cm) pieces
- 1 cup tomatoes, cut into ½-inch (1.5 cm) pieces
- 1 cup bell peppers, cut into ½-inch (1.5 cm) pieces
- 3 tablespoons mint or cilantro leaves, finely chopped
- ⅓ teaspoon salt
- ¼ teaspoon black pepper
- 1 tablespoon lemon juice
- ¾ tablespoon powdered sugar

## Procedure

- Place all the ingredients in a bowl and mix well.

# Beet And Carrot Salad

Preparation time
**12 Min.**

Serves
**2-3 Persons**

## Ingredients

- 2 cups beets, peeled and grated
- 2 cups carrots, peeled and grated
- ⅓ cup celery cut into 1-inch (2.5 cm) pieces
- 2 tablespoons olive oil
- 2 tablespoons lemon juice
- 2 tablespoons pumpkin seeds
- 2 tablespoons sliced almonds
- ⅓ teaspoon salt

## Procedure

Place all the ingredients in a bowl. Mix well.

# Chard And Walnut Salad

Preparation and cooking time
**20 Min.**

Serves
**3-4 Persons**

## Ingredients

- 1 tablespoon oil
- 2 tablespoons sesame seeds
- ⅓ cup walnuts, finely chopped
- 4 cups Swiss or rainbow chard, finely chopped
- 1 teaspoon salt
- ½ teaspoon black pepper
- 1½ teaspoons lemon juice

## Procedure

1. Heat the oil in a frying pan over medium heat. When it is hot but not smoking, add the sesame seeds and cook until they are light brown.

2. Add the walnuts. Continuously stirring, cook until the walnuts turn brown. Add the chard, salt, and pepper. Mix well. Cover the pan. Cook for 4-5 minutes or until the chard reaches to your desired consistency. Stir a few times with a wooden spatula while cooking to make sure the chard is evenly cooked. You can add a little water if needed. Add the lemon juice. Mix well.

# Fruits And Nuts Salad

Chia seeds soaking time
**40-50 Min.**

Preparation and cooking time
**20 Min.**

Serves
**3-4 Persons**

## Ingredients

- 1 cup coconut milk
- 2 tablespoons chia seeds
- ½ cup blueberries
- 1 tablespoon maple syrup
- 1½ tablespoons almond slices
- 1½ tablespoons walnuts, finely chopped
- ¼ teaspoon cinnamon powder
- 2 cups fresh fruits of your choice

## Procedure

1. Place the milk and chia seeds in a blender. Soak them for 40-50 minutes. Add the blueberries and maple syrup. Blend until smooth.

2. Transfer to a bowl. Add the remaining ingredients. Mix gently.

Tahini Salad Dressing

# Tahini Salad Dressing

Preparation and cooking time
**7-8 Min.**

Makes
**1 Cup**

## Ingredients

- ½ cup tahini
- ¾ teaspoon salt
- ¼ teaspoon asafetida
- 2 tablespoons lemon juice
- ⅓ cup (80 ml) water, or as needed

## Procedure

Place all the ingredients in a bowl. Mix with a whisk until a fine paste.

# Walnut And Raisin Salad Dressing

Preparation and cooking time
**10 Min.**

Makes
**1 Cup**

## Ingredients

- ½ cup walnuts
- ¼ cup raisins (adjust to your taste)
- ⅓ teaspoon salt
- ¼ teaspoon asafetida
- 1 tablespoon olive oil
- 1½ tablespoons lemon juice
- ¾ cup (180 ml) + 1 tablespoon water, or as needed

## Procedure

Place all the ingredients in a blender and process to a smooth paste.

# Sadhu Salad Dressing

His Divine Grace Srila Prabhupada inspired his followers to maintain good health and serve Lord Krsna more.

Preparation and cooking time
**12 Min.**

Makes
**2 Cups**

## Ingredients

- ½ tablespoon oil
- ¼ teaspoon asafetida
- 1 tablespoon ginger, peeled and roughly chopped
- ¼ cup sesame seeds
- ¼ cup pumpkin seeds
- ¼ cup sunflower seeds
- 1½ cup (360 ml) water
- 2 tablespoons lemon juice
- 1 teaspoon salt

## Procedure

1. Heat the oil in a frying pan. Add the asafetida and ginger. Continuously stirring, cook for a few seconds. Add the sesame seeds, pumpkin seeds, and sunflower seeds. Continuously stirring, cook over medium heat for 1-2 minutes or until they become light brown. Transfer to a bowl and allow to cool.

2. Transfer to a blender. Add the water, lemon juice, and salt. Blend until smooth.

# Cashew Salad Dressing

Preparation and cooking time
**8 Min.**

Makes
**1 Cup**

## Ingredients

- ½ cup cashew pieces
- ¼ cup white sesame seeds
- ⅓ teaspoon salt
- 1 teaspoon dried basil powder
- ¼ teaspoon asafetida
- ½ teaspoon paprika
- 2 tablespoons olive oil
- ¾ cup (180 ml) water, or as needed

## Procedure

Place all the ingredients in a blender and process them into a smooth paste.

# Celery And Peanut Butter Salad Dressing

Preparation and cooking time
**10 Min.**

Makes
**1½ Cup**

## Ingredients

- 1½ cups celery, cut into small pieces
- 3 tablespoons peanut butter
- 2 tablespoons lemon juice
- ¾ teaspoon salt
- ¼ teaspoon black pepper
- ½ cup (120 ml) water, or as needed

## Procedure

Place all the ingredients in a blender and process to a smooth paste.

# Breads and Mains

# Breads and Mains

Contents

# Breads and Mains

# QUINOA PANCAKE

## Procedure

1. Place the quinoa and enough water in a blender. Blend until a smooth and thick puree like the cake batter consistency. Transfer to a bowl.

2. Add the carrots, salt, black pepper, cumin powder, and parsley. Mix well by using a whisk.

3. Preheat a non-stick, flat griddle. Grease it with a little oil. Pour ½ cup of the batter into the middle of the griddle. Let the batter sit for 4-5 seconds, then place the bottom of a metal measuring cup or a large soup spoon in the center of the batter and pressing lightly, spread the batter outward in a continuous, round motion to make a 6-inch (15 cm) pancake. Cook it for 2-3 minutes or until browned, then carefully turn it over with a spatula. Cook for another 2-3 minutes or until brown spots appear. Repeat the same process until all the pancakes are cooked.

NOTE: you can use oil while cooking.

Preparation and Cooking time
40 Min.

Makes
5 Pancakes

## Ingredients

- 1 cup quinoa
- 1½ cups (360 ml) water, or as needed
- ½ cup carrots, peeled and grated
- 1 teaspoon salt
- ⅓ teaspoon black pepper
- 1 teaspoon cumin powder
- 2tablespoons fresh parsley, finely chopped

# GOPI PANCAKE

The gopis are the cowherd damsels of Sri Vrindavan Dham. Their only desire is to please Lord Kṛṣṇa through their varied loving services, one of which is cooking different preparations with full intent to satisfy Him. The gopis are the most exalted devotees because of their selfless and dedicated service to Lord Kṛṣṇa.

## Ingredients

- 1 cup water chestnut flour
- ½ cup grated, dried coconut
- 2 tablespoons cilantro or mint leaves, finely chopped
- 1 tablespoon green chilies, finely chopped
- 1 teaspoon salt
- 1 teaspoon cumin powder
- 1 cup (240 ml) + 2 tablespoons water, or as needed
- oil for pan frying

## Procedure

1. Combine the water chestnut flour, coconut, cilantro or mint leaves, green chilies, salt, and cumin powder in a bowl. Mix well.

2. Slowly add enough water to make the cake batter-like consistency. Mix well with a whisk.

3. Preheat a non-stick, flat griddle over medium heat. Grease it with little oil. Pour ½ cup of the batter into the middle of the griddle. Let the batter sit for 4-5 seconds, then place the bottom of a metal measuring cup or a large soup spoon in the center of the batter and pressing lightly, spread the batter outward in a continuous, round motion to make a 6-inch (15 cm) pancake. Drizzle 1 teaspoon of oil around the pancake and let it cook for 3-4 minutes or until browned. Carefully turn it over with a spatula and drizzle ½ teaspoon oil over the surface and 1 teaspoon of oil around the edges. Cook for 1-2 minutes or until browned and repeat the same process until all the pancakes are cooked.

Preparation and Cooking time
40 Min.

Makes
5 Pancakes

# STUFFED PANCAKE

## Procedure

1. Place all the ingredients in a blender and process until smooth. You can add a little extra water or quinoa to make the cake batter-like consistency. Transfer to a bowl.

2. Preheat a non-stick griddle over medium heat, then grease it with little oil. Place ½ cup of the batter into the center of the pan. Immediately place a metal measuring cup in the center and lightly spread the batter outward in a continuous spiral motion to 5- inches (12.5 cm) in diameter. Drizzle 1 teaspoon of oil around the pancake and let it cook for 2-3 minutes or until browned. Carefully turn it over with a spatula and drizzle ½ teaspoon oil over the surface and 1 teaspoon of oil around the edges. Cook for 3-4 minutes or until browned.

3. Place one portion of the potato filling in the center of each pancake. Fold both edges to the center. Place on a tray. Repeat the same process until all the pancakes are cooked.

Preparation and Cooking time
40 Min.

Makes
5 Pancakes

## Ingredients

*FILLING*

- 1½ cups potatoes, boiled, peeled, and mashed
- ½ cup carrots, peeled and grated
- ½ cup cabbage, finely shredded
- 1 teaspoon salt
- ½ teaspoon black pepper
- 1½ tablespoons cilantro, finely chopped
- Mix all the ingredients in a bowl. Divide into 5 portions. Set aside.
- 

*PANCAKE*

- 1 cup red quinoa
- ¾ teaspoon salt
- 1 teaspoon cumin powder
- 1 tablespoon green chilies, roughly chopped
- 1¾ cups (420 ml) water, or as needed
- oil for pan-frying

# GREEN PANCAKE

## Procedure

1. Combine the spinach, buckwheat groats, green chilies, ginger root, and a little water in a blender and process until smooth. Transfer to a bowl. You can add extra water to make the cake batter-like consistency.

2. Preheat a non-stick griddle over medium heat, then grease it with little oil. Place ½ cup of the batter into the center of the pan. Immediately place a metal measuring cup in the center and lightly spread the batter outward in a continuous spiral motion to 6- inches (15 cm) in diameter. Drizzle 1 teaspoon of oil around the pancake and let it cook for 3-4 minutes or until browned. Carefully turn it over with a spatula and drizzle ½ teaspoon oil over the surface and 1 teaspoon of oil around the edges. Cook for 3-4 minutes or until browned.

3. Repeat the same process until all the pancakes are cooked.

NOTE: I am not stating the quantity of water in this recipe because spinach becomes very watery after it's ground, so add what you think is the right amount.

## Ingredients

- 4 cups spinach
- 2 cups raw buckwheat groats
- 1½ tablespoons green chilies, roughly chopped
- 1 tablespoon ginger root, peeled and grated
- 1¼ teaspoons salt
- 1 teaspoon cumin powder
- ½ teaspoon asafetida
- water as needed
- oil for pan-frying

Makes
6 Pancakes

Preparation and Cooking time
50 Min.

# ROTI

Another secret ingredient I use while cooking for Sri Sri Radha Golokananda is to listen to Srila Prabhupada's audiobooks, which fill me with energy and enthusiasm.

## Procedure

1. Combine the flours, oil, salt, cilantro, green chili, and cumin seeds in a bowl. Slowly add enough water to make a medium-soft dough and knead for 1-2 minutes. You can grease your palms with oil to make kneading easier.

2. Divide the dough into 8 portions and roll them into balls. Flatten a ball and lightly dip both sides in the dusting flour. Roll it into a thick, 5-inch (12.5 cm) round, dipping it in the dusting flour from time to time, or you can roll the ball between 2 greased zip lock bags.

3. Heat a non-stick flat griddle over medium heat and brush with oil. Gently pick up the roti and place it on the preheated griddle. Cook for approximately 30 seconds-1 minute or until small bubbles begin to form and the bottom has small, light brownish spots. Turn the roti over and cook it on the other side for approximately 1-2 minutes or until the bottom has small brownish spots and is cooked. Turn the roti over again and gently press the top all over with a soft cloth or paper towel, and the roti will slightly puff up. Cook for another 30 seconds-1 minute or until cooked.

4. Remove the roti from the griddle and brush one side with olive or avocado oil. Place the cooked roti into the basket or container and cover. Repeat the same process until all the rotis are cooked.

## Ingredients

- 1 cup amaranth flour
- 1 cup water chestnut flour
- ½ cup buckwheat flour
- 1½ tablespoons oil
- 1¼ teaspoons salt
- ½ cup cilantro, finely chopped
- 1 tablespoon green chilies, finely chopped
- 1 teaspoon cumin seeds
- 1 cup (240 ml) + 1 tablespoon water,
  or as needed
- water chestnut flour for dusting
- olive or avocado oil for brushing the rotis

Makes
8 Rotis

Preparation and Cooking time
45 Min.

# SPINACH ROTI

## Ingredients

- 2 cups spinach
- 1 cup amaranth flour
- 1 cup water chestnut flour
- 1 teaspoon salt
- ⅛ teaspoon black pepper
- 1 teaspoon cumin powder
- 1 tablespoon oil
- water as needed
- water chestnut flour for dusting
- olive or avocado oil for brushing the rotis

Makes
7 Rotis

Preparation and Cooking time
40 Min.

## Procedure

1. Place the spinach and a little water in a blender and process until pureed. Transfer to a bowl. Add the amaranth flour, water chestnut flour, salt, black pepper, and cumin powder. Mix well.

2. Slowly add enough water to make a medium-soft dough and knead for 1-2 minutes. You can grease your palms with oil to make kneading easier.

3. Divide the dough into 7 portions and roll them into balls. Flatten a ball and lightly dip both sides in the dusting flour. Roll it into a thick, 5-inch (12.5 cm) round, dipping it in the dusting flour from time to time, or you can roll the ball between 2 greased zip lock bags.

4. Heat a non-stick flat griddle over medium heat and brush with butter. Gently pick up the roti and place it on the preheated griddle. Cook for 30 seconds-1 minute or until small bubbles begin to form and the bottom has small brown spots. Turn the roti over and cook it the same way for 1-2 minutes or until the bottom has small brown spots. Again turn the roti over and gently press the top with a soft cloth or paper towel, and the roti will slightly puff up. Cook for another 1-1½ minutes or until finished.

5. Remove the roti from the griddle and brush one side with olive oil or avocado oil. Place the cooked roti into a basket or container and cover. Repeat the same process until all the rotis are cooked.

NOTE: I am not stating the quantity of water in this recipe because spinach becomes very watery after it's ground, so add what you think is the right amount.

# SWEET ROTI

The association with Lord Kṛṣṇa's devotees always inspires us to devote our consciousness fully to our devotional services.

Preparation and Cooking time
20 Min.

Makes
3 Rotis

## Procedure

1. Place all the ingredients in a bowl besides water. Mix well. Slowly add enough water to make a medium-soft dough and knead for 1-2 minutes. You can grease your palms with oil to make the kneading easier.

2. Divide the dough into 3 portions and roll them into balls. Flatten a ball and lightly dip both sides in the dusting flour. Roll it into a thick, 4-inch (10 cm) round, dipping it in the dusting flour from time-to-time.

3. Heat a non-stick flat griddle over medium heat and brush it with oil. Gently pick up the roti and place it on the preheated griddle. Cook for approximately 1-2 minutes or until small bubbles begin to form and the bottom has small, light brown spots. Turn the roti over and cook it on the other side for approximately 30 seconds-1 minute or until the bottom has small brown spots and is cooked. Turn the roti over again and gently press the top all over with a soft cloth or paper towel. Cook for another few seconds or until cooked.

4. Remove the roti from the griddle and brush one side with oil. Place the cooked roti into a basket or container and cover. Repeat the same process until all the rotis are cooked.

## Ingredients

- 1 cup amaranth flour
- $\frac{1}{3}$ cup jaggery powder or brown sugar (adjust to your taste)
- $1\frac{1}{2}$ tablespoons white sesame seeds, roasted
- 1 teaspoon oil
- $\frac{1}{3}$ cup (80 ml) water, or as needed
- Amaranth flour for dusting
- olive or avocado oil brushing the rotis

# BROCCOLI PARATHA

## Ingredients

- 1 cup broccoli florets
- 1 tablespoon green chilies, roughly chopped
- 2 cups amaranth flour
- 1 tablespoon oil
- 1¼ teaspoons salt
- 1 teaspoon cumin seeds
- 2 tablespoons cilantro, finely chopped
- ½ cup (120 ml) water, or as needed
- amaranth flour for dusting
- oil for cooking

Makes
6 Parathas

Preparation and Cooking time
40 Min.

## Procedure

1. Blend the broccoli and green chilies in a food processor. Transfer to a bowl.

2. Add the flour, oil, salt, cumin seeds, and cilantro. Mix well. Slowly add enough water to make a medium-soft dough. Knead for 1-2 minutes. You can grease your palms with oil to make kneading easier.

3. Divide the dough into 6 portions and roll them into smooth balls. Flatten each ball and dip both sides lightly in the dusting flour. Roll it into a 6-inch (15 cm) round, dipping it in the dusting flour from time to time, or you can also roll the ball between 2 greased zip lock bags.

4. Preheat a non-stick griddle over medium heat for 2-3 minutes and brush with a little oil. Carefully lay a paratha on the griddle and cook for about 1 minute. Turn it over with a spatula and with a metal tablespoon, drizzle 1 tablespoon of oil on it and ½ tablespoon around the edges. Cook for 1-2 minutes. Adjust the heat so it does not burn. Turn it over again with a spatula and again drizzle 1 tablespoon of oil on it and ½ tablespoon around the edges. Cook for 1-2 minutes. Press the paratha with the spatula while cooking, which helps to make the paratha crisp. The paratha is done when both sides are golden brown and flecked with dark spots. Cook the rest of the parathas in the same way.

# PUMPKIN AND SPINACH PARATHA

## Procedure

1. Heat the oil in a frying pan over medium heat. When it is hot but not smoking, add the pumpkin, salt, turmeric, and ⅓ cup (80 ml) of water. Mix well and cover the frying pan. Occasionally stirring, cook for 3-4 minutes or until the pumpkin is cooked. You can add a little extra water if needed. Transfer to a bowl.

2. Add the cumin seeds, spinach, amaranth flour, water, and chestnut flour. Mix well. Slowly add enough water to make a medium-soft dough. Knead for 1-2 minutes. You can grease your palms with oil to make kneading easier.

3. Divide the dough into 6 portions and roll them into smooth balls. Flatten each ball and dip both sides lightly in the dusting flour. Roll it into a 6-inch (15 cm) round, dipping it in the dusting flour from time to time. You can also roll the ball between 2 greased zip lock bags.

4. Preheat a non-stick griddle over medium heat for 2-3 minutes and brush with a little oil. Carefully lay a paratha on the griddle and cook for about 1 minute. Turn it over with a spatula and with a metal tablespoon, drizzle 1 tablespoon of oil on it, and ½ tablespoon around the edges. Cook for 1-2 minutes. Adjust the heat so it does not burn. Turn it over again with a spatula and again drizzle 1 tablespoon of oil on it and ½ tablespoon around the edges. Cook for 1-2 minutes. Press the paratha with the spatula while cooking, which helps to make the paratha crisp. The paratha is done when both sides are golden brown and flecked with dark spots. Cook the rest of the parathas in the same way.

## Ingredients

- 1½ tablespoons oil
- ¾ cup pumpkin, peeled, seeded, and grated
- 1¼ teaspoons salt
- 1 teaspoon turmeric
- 1 teaspoon cumin seeds
- 1 cup spinach, finely chopped
- 1 cup amaranth flour
- 1 cup water chestnut flour
- ⅓ cup (80 ml) + ½ cup (120 ml) water, or as needed
- amaranth flour for dusting
- oil for cooking

Makes
6 Parathas

Preparation and Cooking time
45 Min.

# BEET PURI

Preparation and Cooking time
25 Min.

Makes
12 Puris

## Ingredients

- 1 cup amaranth flour
- 1 cup water chestnut flour
- ¾ cup beets, peeled and grated
- ½ cup cilantro, finely chopped
- 2 tablespoons oil
- 1¼ teaspoons salt
- 1¼ teaspoons cumin seeds
- ½ cup (120 ml) + 1 tablespoon water, or as needed
- oil for deep-frying

## Procedure

1. Combine the flours, beets, cilantro, oil, salt, and cumin seeds in a bowl. Mix well.

2. Slowly add enough water to make a firm dough. Knead for 1-2 minutes. You can grease your palms with oil to make kneading easier. Divide the dough into 12 portions and roll them into smooth balls. Roll each ball into a 4-inch (10 cm) round on a greased working surface, or you can roll it out after dipping the ball into the dry flour. Place on a greased tray. Repeat until all the puris are rolled.

3. Heat the oil in a 2½-inch (6.5 cm) deep frying pan until the temperature reaches 325°F (162°C).

4. Carefully slip a puri into the hot oil. The puri will sink for a second, then rise to the surface and sputter. As soon as it does this, take a slotted spoon and swiftly keep pushing it back down until it puffs, then carefully turn it over and cook it on the other side. The frying time is about 1 minute for both sides. Remove the puri from the oil with the slotted spoon and drain on paper towels. Repeat the process for all the puris. If the puri does not rise to the surface immediately, then the oil is not hot enough.

# CUCUMBER PURI

Preparation and Cooking time
25 Min.

Makes
12 Puris

## Procedure

1. Combine the flour, cucumber, oil, salt, cumin powder, and sesame seeds in a bowl. Mix well.

2. Slowly add enough water to make a firm dough. Knead for 1-2 minutes. You can grease your palms with oil to make kneading easier. Divide the dough into 12 portions and roll them into smooth balls. On a greased working surface, or by dipping the ball into the dry flour, roll each ball into a 4-inch (10 cm) round. Place on a greased tray. Repeat until all the puris are rolled. Heat the oil in a 2½-inch (6.5 cm) deep frying pan until the temperature reaches 325°F (162°C).

3. Lift a puri and carefully slip it into the hot oil. The puri will sink for a second, then rise to the surface and sputter. As soon as it does this, take a slotted spoon and swiftly keep pushing it back down until it puffs. When it is cooked on the first side, carefully turn it over and cook it on the other side. The frying time is about 1 minute for both sides. Remove the puri from the oil with a slotted spoon and drain on paper towels. Repeat the process for all the puris. If the puri does not rise to the surface immediately, then the oil is not hot enough.

## Ingredients

- 2 cups buckwheat flour
- ½ cup cucumber peeled and grated
- 1 tablespoon oil
- 1¼ teaspoons salt
- 1 teaspoon cumin powder
- 2 tablespoons white sesame seeds
- ½ cup (120 ml) + 1 tablespoon water, or as needed
- oil for deep-frying

# BREAD BUNS

Preparation time: 15 Min.
Baking time: 25-30 Min.

Makes
5 Buns

## Ingredients

- 1 cup almond flour
- 1 cup ground flax seeds
- 1 teaspoon salt
- 2 tablespoons white sesame seeds
- ⅓ teaspoon baking soda
- 1 tablespoon oil
- ⅓ cup (80 ml) water, or as needed

## Procedure

1. Place all the ingredients except the water in a bowl. Mix well. Slowly add enough water to make a medium-soft dough and knead for 1-2 minutes. You can grease your palms with oil to make the kneading easier.

2. Divide the dough into 5 portions and roll them into smooth balls. Slightly flatten between your palms.

3. Place them on a greased baking tray. Bake in a preheated oven at 350°F (177°C) for 25-30 minutes or until the tops turn light brown.

# VEGAN GAURANGA POTATO

## Procedure

1. Combine the sunflower seeds, ginger root, sunflower oil, and water in a blender. Blend until smooth. Transfer to a bowl.

2. Add the salt, turmeric, asafetida, black pepper, and rosemary. Mix well. Mix the potatoes in so they are evenly coated with the paste.

3. Transfer to a greased 9 x 13 x 2 inches (22.5 x 32.5 x 5 cm) baking pan. Sprinkle the paprika on top of the potato mixture.

4. Bake the potatoes in the preheated oven at 350°F (177°C) for 30-35 minutes or until the potatoes are cooked, and the top part is brown.

Preparation time: About 15 min.
Baking time: 30-35 min.

Serves
4-5 Persons

## Ingredients

- 1¼ cups sunflower seeds
- 1 tablespoon ginger root, peeled and roughly chopped
- 2 tablespoons oil
- 1½ cups (360 ml) water, or as needed
- 1½ teaspoons salt
- 2½ teaspoons turmeric
- ½ teaspoon asafetida
- ¼ teaspoon black pepper
- ½ teaspoon dried rosemary
- 4 cups potatoes, peeled and cut into thin slices
- ⅓ teaspoon paprika

# RAMA QUINOA

Lord Rama means the one who gives pleasure to others. My husband and friends were so happy with this particular preparation that I decided to name this dish after Him.

Preparation and Cooking time
40 Min.

Serves
3-4 Persons

## Ingredients

- 2 tablespoons oil
- ½ cup peanuts or cashews, finely chopped
- ½ cup potatoes peeled and cut into ½-inch (1.5 cm) pieces
- ½ cup bell peppers, cut into ½-inch
(1.5 cm) pieces
- ½ cup broccoli, cut into ½-inch (1.5 cm) florets
- ½ cup carrots peeled and cut into ½-inch (1.5 cm)
- 1 teaspoon salt
- ⅓ teaspoon cayenne pepper
- 1½ teaspoons turmeric
- 1½ teaspoons coriander powder
- 2 cups cooked quinoa

## Procedure

1. Heat the oil in a non-stick frying-pan pan over medium heat. Add the peanuts or cashews. Continuously stirring, cook for 1-2 minutes or until golden brown.

2. Add the potatoes, bell peppers, broccoli, carrots, salt, cayenne pepper, turmeric, and coriander powder. Cover the pan and cook for 12-15 minutes or until the vegetables become tender. Stir a few times with a wooden spatula while cooking to make sure the vegetables are evenly cooked.

3. Add the quinoa. Mix well.

# SAMO PULAO

Samo is seed and grain-free. It's also known as moriyo or samak rice and is available at Indian grocery stores.

## Procedure

1. Heat the oil in a pressure cooker over medium heat. When it is hot but not smoking, add the cumin seeds and sauté until lightly brown. Add the ginger and green chili. Continuously stirring, cook for a few seconds. Add the water. Cook until the water starts to boil. Add the samo, salt, and black pepper. Mix well and place the lid on the cooker. Pressure cook for 2 whistles over medium-high heat.

2. Turn off the heat and remove the pressure cooker from the stove. Wait until all the steam has escaped before opening it.

3. Heat the oil in a 2½-inch (6.5 cm) deep frying pan until the temperature reaches 300°F (148°C). Place the potatoes in the oil without crowding them and fry for 5-6 minutes or until golden brown on both sides. Remove the potatoes with a slotted spoon and place them on a paper towel to absorb the extra oil.

4. Place the cashews in the oil without crowding them and fry for 30 seconds-1 minute or until golden brown on both sides. Remove the cashews with a slotted spoon and place them on a paper towel to absorb the extra oil.

5. Add to the cooked samo. Mix well.

NOTE: Samo absorbs the water after a little while. You can add extra hot water if needed.

## Ingredients

- 1 tablespoon oil
- 1 teaspoon cumin seeds
- 1 tablespoon ginger root, peeled and grated
- 1 tablespoon green chili, finely chopped
- 4 cups (960 ml) water
- 1 cup samo
- 1 teaspoon salt
- ⅓ teaspoon black pepper
- 1¾ cups potatoes peeled and finely chopped
- ¾ cup cashews
- oil for deep frying

Serves
3-4 Persons

Preparation and Cooking time
30 Min.

# BUCKWHEAT PULAO

Preparation and Cooking time
35 Min.

Serves
3-4 Persons

## Ingredients

- 2½ cups (600 ml) water, or as needed
- 1 cup raw buckwheat groats
- 2 teaspoons salt
- 2 tablespoons oil
- 1 teaspoon cumin seeds
- 1 tablespoon ginger root, peeled and grated
- 1 tablespoon green chili, finely chopped
- ¾ cup eggplant, cut into 1½-inch pieces
- ¾ cup sweet potatoes peeled and cut into 1½-inch pieces
- ¾ cup bell peppers, cut into 1½-inch pieces
- ¾ cup broccoli cut into 2-inch florets
- ¼ teaspoon black pepper
- 1½ tablespoons white sesame seeds
- 1½ tablespoons peanuts or almonds, ground
- ¾ cup cilantro, finely chopped
- 2 tablespoons lemon juice

## Procedure

1. Boil the water in a 3-quart saucepan over medium-high heat. Add the buckwheat and 1 teaspoon of salt. Cover the pan and cook over medium heat for 15-20 minutes or until the buckwheat is cooked. While cooking, stir a few times with a wooden spatula to ensure it does not stick to the bottom of the pan and is evenly cooked. You can add extra water if needed.

2. Heat the oil in a non-stick frying pan over medium heat. When it is hot but not smoking, add the cumin seeds and sauté until they turn brown. Add the ginger root and green chili. Continuously stirring, cook for a few seconds.

3. Add the eggplant, sweet potatoes, bell peppers, broccoli, black pepper, and the remaining salt (1 teaspoon). Cover the pan. Cook over medium heat for 7-8 minutes. Add the sesame seeds, peanuts or almonds, and cilantro. Cover the pan. Cook over medium heat for 5-6 minutes more or until the vegetables are cooked. Stir a few times with a wooden spatula while cooking to make sure the vegetables do not stick to the bottom and it is evenly cooked. Add the buckwheat and lemon juice. Mix gently.

# BAKED POTATOES IN SPINACH SAUCE

Preparation and cooking time: 25 min.
Baking time: 12-15 min.

Serves
3-4 Persons

## Ingredients

- 2 cups potatoes, peeled and cut into 1-inch (2.5 cm) pieces
- 1 tablespoon oil
- 3 cups spinach
- ¼ cup (60 ml) water
- 2 cups tomatoes, roughly chopped
- 1 tablespoon ginger root, peeled and roughly chopped
- 1 tablespoon green chilies, roughly chopped
- ½ teaspoon salt
- ⅛ teaspoon black pepper

## Procedure

1. Place the potatoes and oil into a bowl. Mix well. Transfer to a greased baking tray.

2. Bake the potatoes in a preheated oven at 350°F (177°C) for 12-15 minutes or until the potatoes are done.

3. Place the spinach and water in a 3-quart saucepan. Cook uncovered over medium heat for 3-4 minutes or until the spinach is cooked. Allow to cool. Place the spinach, tomatoes, ginger root, and green chilies into a blender and process to a smooth puree. Transfer to a 3-quart saucepan.

4. Add the salt and black pepper. Occasionally stirring, cook on medium-high heat for 7-8 minutes or until the desired consistency. Add the potatoes and mix gently.

# BAKED VEGETABLES

Preparation and cooking time: 20 min.
Baking time: 30-40 min.

Serves
4-5 Persons

## Ingredients

- 1 cup potatoes, peeled and cut into thin slices
- 1 cup sweet potatoes, peeled and cut into thin slices
- 1 cup zucchini, cut into thin slices
- 1 cup eggplant, cut into thin slices
- 1 cup carrots, peeled and cut into thin slices
- 1 cup Brussels sprouts, cut into thin slices
- 3 tablespoons oil
- 1 teaspoon salt
- ⅓ teaspoon asafetida
- 3 tablespoons fresh rosemary, finely chopped
- 2 tablespoons lemon juice

## Procedure

1. Place all the ingredients in a bowl. Mix well.

2. Transfer to a greased 9 x 13 x 2 inch (22.5 x 32.5 x 5 cm) baking pan. Cover with aluminum foil.

3. Bake the vegetables in a preheated oven at 350°F (177°C) for 20-25 minutes. Remove the foil. Bake uncovered for 10-15 minutes more or until the vegetables are tender.

# BAKED POTATOES

Preparation time: 10 min.
Baking time: 15-20 min.

Serves
2-3 Persons

## Procedure

1. Cut the potatoes into 2-inch cubes. Place in a bowl and add the remaining ingredients. Mix well.

2. Place in a greased baking tray. Bake at 350°F (177°C) for 20 minutes. Take out the tray from the oven. Turn over the potatoes. Bake for 20-25 minutes more or until the top part is browned.

## Ingredients

- 4-5 medium-sized, parboiled potatoes, unpeeled
- 1 teaspoon salt
- ½ teaspoon freshly ground black pepper
- ¼ teaspoon asafetida
- ¾ tablespoon dried rosemary
- 4 tablespoons oil

# BAKED SWEET POTATOES

Preparation time: 10 min.
Baking time: 15-20 min.

Serves
2-3 Persons

## Procedure

1. Place all the ingredients in a bowl. Mix well. Transfer to a greased baking tray.

2. Bake the sweet potatoes in the preheated oven at 350°F (177°C) for 15-20 minutes or until they become tender.

## Ingredients

- 3 cups sweet potatoes, peeled and cut into 1-inch (2.5 cm) pieces
- ⅓ teaspoon salt
- ¼ teaspoon cayenne pepper
- ½ teaspoon cumin powder
- 1 teaspoon dried basil powder
- a pinch of black pepper
- ¼ teaspoon asafetida
- 2 teaspoons oil

Preparation time: 7 min.
Baking time: 30 min.

Serves
2-3 Persons

# BAKED BRUSSELS SPROUTS AND CASHEWS

## Ingredients

- ½ lb. (226 gm) Brussels sprouts
- 1 tablespoon oil
- ⅓ teaspoon salt
- ¼ teaspoon paprika
- ½ teaspoon dried rosemary
- ¾ cup cashew pieces, raw and unsalted

## Procedure

1. Wash the Brussels sprouts and pat dry. Cut off the top where the stem was and peel off the top few leaves. Cut each Brussels sprout into half lengthwise and then into quarters.

2. Transfer to a bowl. Add the oil, salt, paprika, and rosemary. Mix well. Transfer to a greased baking tray.

3. Bake the Brussels sprouts in the preheated oven at 350°F (177°C) for 25-30 minutes or until they become tender. Transfer to a bowl.

4. Place the cashews on a greased baking tray. Bake the cashew pieces in preheated oven at 350°F (177°C) for 7-8 minutes or until they are light brown. Mix well into the Brussels sprouts.

Stuffed Bell Peppers

# STUFFED BELL PEPPERS

Preparation and cooking time: 25 min.
Baking time: 12-15 min.

Serves
2 Persons

## Ingredients

- 2 medium-sized bell peppers
- 1 tablespoon oil
- ½ cup walnuts, finely chopped
- ½ carrot, peeled and grated
- 1 cup spinach, finely chopped
- 1 cup cooked quinoa
- ¾ teaspoon salt
- ⅓ teaspoon black pepper
- 1 teaspoon cumin powder
- 1 tablespoon lemon juice

## Procedure

1. Cut off the top of the bell peppers. Scoop out the seeds and rinse out any remaining seeds. Set them aside.

2. Heat the oil in a non-stick frying pan over medium heat. Add the walnuts. Continuously stirring, cook for 30 seconds-1 minute or until they become golden brown.

3. Add the carrots and spinach. Occasionally stirring, cook for 3-4 minutes or until the vegetables become tender. Add the quinoa, salt, black pepper, cumin powder, and lemon juice. Mix well.

4. Carefully stuff the bell peppers with the quinoa and vegetables and replace the tops. Place them on a greased baking tray.

5. Bake the bell peppers in a preheated oven at 350°F (177°C) for 12-15 minutes or until the bell peppers become tender.

# ASPARAGUS WITH WALNUTS

I'm very appreciative of my husband, Gopal Das, for encouraging me to engage in this cooking service for Lord Kṛṣṇa.

Preparation and Cooking time
15 Min.

Serves
2-3 Persons

## Ingredients

- 1 tablespoon oil
- 1 teaspoon cumin seeds
- ¼ cup ground walnuts
- 2 cups fresh asparagus, trimmed and cut into 2-inch (5 cm) pieces
- ½ teaspoon salt
- ¼ teaspoon black pepper
- 1 tablespoon lemon juice

## Procedure

1. Heat the oil in a frying pan over medium heat. When it is hot but not smoking, add the cumin seeds and sauté until they turn brown.

2. Add the walnuts, asparagus, salt, and black pepper. Continuously stirring, cook for about 4-5 minutes or until the asparagus is cooked but still a little crunchy. Add the lemon juice.

# ZUCCHINI KOFTA IN TOMATO SAUCE

This recipe is appreciated by Priya Ghatwai very much, who is the tester and taster of most of the recipes in this cookbook.

## Ingredients

***KOFTA***

- 2 cups zucchini, shredded
- ½ cup water chestnut flour
- ¾ teaspoon salt
- ¼ teaspoon black pepper
- 1½ tablespoons ginger root, peeled and grated
- 2 tablespoons cilantro, finely chopped

***SAUCE***

- ½ cup blanched peanuts
- 2 tablespoons oil
- 2 cups tomato puree made from fresh tomatoes
- ¾ teaspoon salt
- ⅓ teaspoon cayenne pepper
- ½ teaspoon turmeric
- 1 teaspoon coriander powder
- ¾ teaspoon cumin powder

## Procedure

***KOFTA***

1. Squeeze the water from the shredded zucchini. Transfer to a bowl. Add the flour, salt, black pepper, ginger root, and cilantro. Mix well. Divide the mixture into 10 portions and roll each portion into a ball. Place on a greased baking tray.

2. Bake the koftas in the preheated oven at 350°F (177°C) for 15-20 minutes or until they are light brown, then allow them to cool. Carefully remove the koftas from the baking tray with a knife.

***SAUCE***

1. Place the peanuts and a little water in a blender and process until smooth.

2. Heat the oil in a non-stick frying pan over medium heat. Add the peanut paste. Continuously stirring, cook for 4-5 minutes. Add the tomato puree, salt, cayenne pepper, turmeric, coriander powder, and cumin powder. Occasionally stirring, cook for 8-10 minutes over medium heat or until the desired consistency. Place the koftas in the sauce 5 minutes before serving.

Preparation and cooking time: 20 min.
Baking time: 15-20 min.

Serves
5-6 Persons

# MIXED VEGETABLE KOFTA SABJI

His Grace Apurva Das, one of the most accomplished cooks in our ISKCON movement, told me that to have the best consciousness while cooking, I should chant:

Hare Kṛṣṇa Hare Kṛṣṇa
Kṛṣṇa Kṛṣṇa Hare Hare
Hare Rama Hare Rama
Rama Rama Hare Hare

Preparation and cooking time: 25 min.
Baking time: about 15-20 min.

Serves
5-6 Persons

## Ingredients

***KOFTA***

- 2 cups potatoes, boiled, peeled, and mashed
- 1 cup spinach, finely chopped
- 1 cup cabbage, finely shredded
- ½ cup carrot, peeled and grated
- ¾ cup amaranth flour
- 1¼ teaspoons salt
- 1 tablespoon ginger root, peeled and grated
- 1 tablespoon green chilies, finely chopped
- 2 tablespoons cilantro, finely chopped

***SAUCE***

- 1 tablespoon oil
- 3 cups tomato puree made from fresh tomatoes
- 1 cup coconut milk
- 1 teaspoon salt
- ⅓ teaspoon cayenne pepper
- 1½ teaspoons coriander powder
- 1 teaspoon cumin powder

## Procedure

***KOFTA***

1. Place all the ingredients in a bowl. Mix well. Divide into 12 portions and roll each portion into a ball. You can add a little water if the mixture is too dry. Place on a greased baking tray.

2. Bake the koftas in the preheated oven at 350°F (177°C) for 15-20 minutes or until they become light brown, then allow them to cool. Carefully remove the koftas from the baking tray with a knife.

***SAUCE***

Heat the oil in a frying pan. Add the tomato puree. Occasionally stirring, cook for 8-10 minutes. Add the coconut milk, salt, cayenne pepper, coriander powder, and cumin powder.
Occasionally stirring, cook for 4-5 minutes or until it reaches the desired consistency. Place the koftas in the sauce for 2-3 minutes before serving.

Mixed Vegetable Kofta Sabji

# POTATO AND SWEET POTATO SABJI

## Procedure

1. Heat the oil in a non-stick frying pan over medium heat. When it is hot but not smoking, add the cumin seeds and sauté until they turn brown.

2. Add the ginger root and green chilies. Continuously stirring, cook for a few seconds. Add the potatoes and salt. Cover the pan and cook over medium heat for 15-18 minutes or until the vegetables become tender. Stir a few times with a wooden spatula while cooking to make sure it does not stick to the bottom, and the vegetables are evenly cooked.

3. Turn off the heat. Add the cilantro and coconut. Cover the pan for 3-4 minutes, then mix gently.

Preparation and Cooking time
30 Min.

Serves
2-3 Persons

## Ingredients

- 1½ tablespoons coconut oil
- 2 teaspoons cumin seeds
- ¾ tablespoon ginger root, peeled and grated
- ¾ tablespoon green chilies, finely chopped
- 1½ cups potatoes peeled and cut into 1-inch (2.5 cm) pieces
- 1½ cups sweet potatoes peeled and cut into 1-inch (2.5 cm) pieces
- 1 teaspoon salt
- ⅓ cup cilantro, finely chopped
- 1 tablespoon grated, dried coconut

# CAULIFLOWER AND SPINACH SABJI

Preparation and cooking time: 15 min.
Baking time: 15-20 min.

Serves
3-4 Persons

## Ingredients

- 4 cups cauliflower cut into 1-inch (2.5 cm) florets
- 2 teaspoon oil
- 1¼ teaspoons salt
- ½ teaspoon cayenne pepper
- ¾ teaspoon turmeric
- 1½ teaspoons coriander powder

***SAUCE***

- 2 teaspoons oil
- ⅓ teaspoon asafetida
- 3 tablespoons white sesame seeds
- 4 cups spinach, finely chopped

## Procedure

1. Place all the ingredients in a bowl and toss to coat with the spices.

2. Place the cauliflower in a single layer on a greased 9 x 13-inch (22.5 x 32.5 cm) baking tray. Bake the cauliflower in a preheated oven at 350°F (177°C) for 20-25 minutes or until cooked. Transfer to a bowl.

***SAUCE***

1. Heat the oil in a frying pan over medium heat. When it is hot but not smoking, add the asafetida. Cook for a few seconds.

2. Add the sesame seeds. Continuously stirring, cook for 1-2 minutes until they become light brown.

3. Add the spinach. Continuously stirring, cook for 2-3 minutes or until tender. Mix gently with the cauliflower.

# OKRA SABJI

## Procedure

1. Wash the okra and dry them thoroughly with a paper towel. Cut off the ends and dice into ¼-inch (6 mm) rounds.

2. Separately dry roast the peanuts and sesame seeds. Grind them together.

3. Heat the oil in a non-stick frying pan. When it is hot but not smoking, add the asafetida and fry for a few seconds.

4. Add the okra, salt, cayenne pepper, and coriander powder. Cook uncovered over medium heat for 20-25 minutes or until the okra is tender. Stir a few times while cooking to make sure it cooks evenly. Add the sesame seeds and peanuts. Mix gently.

Preparation and Cooking time
35 Min.

Serves
3-4 Persons

## Ingredients

- 1 lb. (453 gm) okra
- 3 tablespoons oil
- ¼ teaspoon asafetida
- ¾ teaspoon salt
- ⅓ teaspoon cayenne pepper
- 1 teaspoon coriander powder
- 2 tablespoons peanuts
- 2 tablespoons white sesame seeds

# EGGPLANT AND POTATO SABJI

Srila Prabhupada, the Founder Acarya of the ISKCON movement, was an excellent cook and inspired his followers to cook for Lord Kṛṣṇa.

## Ingredients

- 3 cups eggplant, cut into ½ -inch (1.27 cm) slices
- 3 cups potatoes, peeled and cut into ½ -inch (1.27 cm) slices
- 1 teaspoon oil
- 1 teaspoon cumin seeds
- 2 cups tomato puree made from fresh tomatoes
- ¾ teaspoon salt
- 1 teaspoon turmeric
- ½ teaspoon cayenne pepper
- 1½ teaspoons coriander powder
- 1½ tablespoons cilantro, finely chopped
- oil for pan-frying

Preparation and Cooking time
45 Min.

Serves
3-4 Persons

## Procedure

1. Heat a non-stick frying pan over medium heat and add enough oil to coat the bottom. Place the eggplant slices in the pan without crowding them.

2. Cook over medium heat for 4-5 minutes or until golden brown on one side. Carefully turn them over and cook for 3-4 minutes or until browned. Transfer to a bowl.

3. Place the potato slices in the pan without crowding them. Cook over medium heat for 6-8 minutes or until golden brown on one side. Carefully turn them over and cook for 4-6 minutes or until browned. Transfer to the bowl of eggplant.

4. Heat the oil in a frying pan over medium heat. When it is hot but not smoking, add the cumin seeds and sauté until they turn brown.

5. Add the tomato puree, salt, turmeric, cayenne pepper, and coriander powder. Frequently stirring, cook for 5-7 minutes or until the desired consistency.

6. Add the eggplant and potato slices. Cook for 1-2 minutes. Garnish with cilantro.

# BROCCOLI AND SWEET POTATO SABJI

## Procedure

1. Combine the sesame seeds, cashew pieces, tomatoes, and black peppercorns in a blender and process to a smooth paste. You can add a little water if required.

2. Heat the oil in a non-stick frying pan over medium heat. When it is hot but not smoking, add the asafetida. Continuously stirring, cook for a few seconds.

3. Add the paste. Continuously stirring, cook for 7-8 minutes. Add sweet potatoes, salt, cumin powder, coriander powder, coconut milk, and water. Cover the pan and cook for about 5-7 minutes.

4. Add the broccoli. Cover the pan and cook for 12-15 minutes or until the vegetables become tender. Stir a few times with a wooden spatula while cooking to make sure the vegetables do not stick to the bottom of the pan and are evenly cooked.

## Ingredients

- ½ cup white sesame seeds
- ½ cup cashew pieces
- 1 cup tomatoes, roughly chopped
- ⅓ teaspoon peppercorns
- 2 tablespoons oil
- ¼ teaspoon asafetida
- 2 cups sweet potatoes, peeled and cut into 1-inch (2.5 cm) pieces
- 1¼ teaspoons salt
- 1 teaspoon cumin powder
- 1 teaspoon coriander powder
- ¾ cup coconut milk
- ¾ cup (180 ml) water
- 2 cups broccoli, cut into ¾-inch (2 cm) florets

Preparation and Cooking time
40 Min.

Serves
4-5 Persons

# BRUSSELS SPROUTS SABJI

Preparation and cooking time: 25 min.
Baking time: 20-25 min.

Serves
5-6 Persons

## Ingredients

- 3 medium-sized red bell peppers
- 1 medium-sized eggplant
- 2 medium-sized tomatoes, cut into medium-sized pieces
- 1 tablespoon oil
- 1½ teaspoons salt
- 3 cups steamed Brussels sprouts

## Procedure

1. Preheat the oven to 350°F (177°C). Place the bell peppers and eggplant on a greased baking tray. Bake the vegetables for 20-25 minutes or until tender, then allow them to cool.

2. Remove the skin and seeds from bell peppers and eggplant and cut them into small pieces. Transfer to a blender. Add the tomato pieces and blend until a smooth paste.

3. Heat the oil in a frying pan. Add the paste. Occasionally stirring, cook for 12-15 minutes or until the desired consistency. Add the salt and the Brussels sprouts. Mix well.

NOTE: If you like, you can thinly slice the Brussels sprouts before or after steaming. You can also use steamed broccoli, cauliflower, or baby potatoes instead of Brussels sprouts.

# BELL PEPPER SABJI

Preparation and Cooking time
25 Min.

Serves
2-3 Persons

## Procedure

1. Heat the oil in a non-stick frying pan over medium heat. When it is hot but not smoking, add the bell peppers, green chilies, and ginger root. Continuously stirring, cook for 1-2 minutes.

2. Add the salt and cumin powder. Continuously stirring, cook for 1-2 minutes.

3. Add the coconut, sesame seeds, peanuts, cilantro, and water. Cover the pan and cook for 6-8 minutes over medium heat or until the bell peppers are tender. Stir a few times with a wooden spatula while cooking to make sure the sabji does not stick and it is evenly cooked.

## Ingredients

- 1 tablespoon oil
- 2 cups bell peppers, cut into 1-inch (2.5 cm) pieces
- ½ tablespoon green chilies, finely chopped
- ½ tablespoon ginger root, peeled and finely chopped
- ¾ teaspoon salt
- 1½ teaspoons cumin powder
- 1 tablespoon grated, dried coconut
- ½ tablespoon white sesame seeds
- 1 tablespoon peanuts, ground
- ½ cup cilantro, finely chopped
- 2 tablespoons water

# CASHEW AND SPINACH SABJI

Preparation and Cooking time
25 Min.

Serves
2-3 Persons

## Ingredients

- 3 cups tomatoes, roughly chopped
- 2 tablespoons white sesame seeds
- 2 tablespoons grated, dried coconut
- 2 tablespoons oil
- ½ cup cashews, finely chopped
- ¾ teaspoon salt
- ¼ teaspoon cayenne powder
- 1 teaspoon cumin powder
- 3 cups spinach, finely chopped

## Procedure

1. Place the tomatoes, sesame seeds, and coconut in a blender. Blend till a smooth puree.

2. Heat 1 tablespoon oil in a frying pan over medium heat. Add the cashews. Continuously stirring, cook for about 1 minute or until light brown. Transfer to a bowl.

3. Heat the remaining (1 tablespoon) oil in a frying pan. Add the tomato puree, salt, cayenne pepper, and cumin powder. Occasionally stirring, cook for 5-7 minutes over medium-high heat or until the desired consistency.

4. Add the cashews and spinach. Cook over medium-high heat, uncovered for 4-5 minutes or until the spinach is tender. Stir a few times while cooking.

# ALMOND AND YELLOW SQUASH SABJI

Almond soaking time: 20-25 min.
Preparation and cooking time: 20 min.

Serves
3-4 Persons

## Procedure

1. Place the almonds and boiling water in a bowl. Cover and soak for 20-25 minutes. Drain the water and peel off the skin.

2. Heat the oil in a frying pan over medium heat. When it is hot but not smoking, add the cumin seeds and sauté until they turn brown. Add the green chilies and ginger root. Continuously stirring, cook for a few seconds.

3. Add the yellow squash, salt, black pepper, water, and almonds. Cover the pan. Cook over medium heat for 8-10 minutes or until the vegetable is tender. Stir a few times with a wooden spatula while cooking to make sure the sabji is evenly cooked.

4. Add the cilantro. Cook for 2-3 minutes, uncovered over medium heat. Add the lemon juice.

## Ingredients

- ⅓ cup almonds
- 1½ cups (360 ml) boiling water
- 1 tablespoon oil
- 1 teaspoon cumin seeds
- ¾ tablespoon green chilies, finely chopped
- ¾ tablespoon ginger root, peeled and grated
- 3 cups yellow squash, cut into 1½-inch (4 cm) pieces
- ¾ teaspoon salt
- ⅛ teaspoon black pepper
- ⅓ cup (80 ml) water, or as needed
- ½ cup cilantro, finely chopped
- 1 teaspoon lemon juice

# PLANTAIN SABJI

## Ingredients

- 2½ cups plantains peeled and cut into ¼-inch (6mm) slices
- 3 cups tomatoes, roughly chopped
- 1 cup cucumber, peeled and roughly chopped
- 2 tablespoons grated, dried coconut
- 1 tablespoon green chili, roughly chopped
- 1 tablespoon ginger root, peeled and roughly chopped
- 1 tablespoon oil
- 1 teaspoon cumin seeds
- 1½ teaspoons salt
- 1 teaspoon turmeric
- ⅛ teaspoon cayenne pepper
- oil for deep frying

## Procedure

1. Heat the oil in a 2½-inch (6.5 cm) deep frying pan over medium heat until the temperature reaches 250°F (121°C). Carefully place the plantain slices into the hot oil without crowding them. Fry for 4-5 minutes or until golden brown, then turn them over. Maintaining a temperature of 250°F (121°C) to 300°F (148°C), fry for 3-4 minutes more.

2. Remove them with a slotted spoon and place them on a paper towel to absorb the extra oil.

3. Combine the tomatoes, cucumber, coconut, green chili, and ginger root in a blender. Blend until it becomes a smooth puree.

4. Heat the oil in a frying pan over medium heat. When it is hot but not smoking, add the cumin seeds and sauté until they turn brown.

5. Add the tomato puree, salt, turmeric, coriander powder, and cayenne pepper. Frequently stirring, cook over medium heat for 8-10 minutes or until the desired consistency. Add the plantain chips. Cook over medium heat for 2-3 minutes more.

Serves
4-5 Persons

Preparation and Cooking time
25 Min.

# APPETIZERS AND ACCOMPANIMENTS

# APPETIZERS AND ACCOMPANIMENTS

# Potato Kofta

**Preparation and cooking time**

25 Min.

**Makes**

12 kofta balls

## Ingredients

- 2 cups potatoes, boiled, peeled, and mashed
- ⅓ cup peanuts, ground
- ⅓ cup almonds
- 1 tablespoon green chilies, finely chopped
- 1 tablespoon ginger root, peeled and grated
- 2 tablespoons cilantro, finely chopped
- 1¼ teaspoons salt
- ½ cup water chestnut flour
- oil for deep-frying

## Procedure

1. Mix all the ingredients in a bowl. Divide into 12 portions and roll into smooth balls. Place on a greased tray.

2. Heat the oil in a 2½-inch (6.5 cm) deep frying pan until the temperature reaches 300°F (148°C). Carefully place the koftas into the oil without crowding them. Fry for 4-5 minutes or until golden brown, then turn them over. Maintaining a temperature of 300°F (148°C) to 325°F (162°C), fry them for another 3-4 minutes or until golden brown on both sides.

3. Remove the koftas with a slotted spoon and place them on a paper towel to absorb the extra oil.

# Broccoli Pakora

**Preparation and cooking time**

25 Min.

**Serves**

4-5 Persons

## Ingredients

- 1 cup buckwheat flour
- 1 teaspoon salt
- ⅓ teaspoon cayenne pepper
- 1 teaspoon coriander powder
- 2 tablespoons white sesame seeds
- 1½ cups (360 ml) water, or as needed
- 2 cups broccoli, cut into 1½-inch (4 cm) florets
- oil for deep-frying

## Procedure

1. Combine the buckwheat flour, salt, cayenne pepper, coriander powder, and sesame seeds in a bowl. Slowly add enough water and mix with a whisk until a thick batter-like consistency.

2. Heat the oil in a 2½-inch (6.5 cm) deep frying pan until the temperature reaches 300°F (148°C). Dip the broccoli florets in the batter and make sure they are completely covered. Carefully place the pakoras into the oil without crowding them. Fry for 3-4 minutes or until cooked, then turn them over and maintain a temperature of 300°F (148°C) to 325°F (162°C); fry for 2-3 minutes more or until finished.

3. Remove the pakoras with a slotted spoon and place them on a paper towel to absorb the extra oil.

# Potato Pakora

My sincere gratitude goes to my talented mother, Srimati Maina Devi, for devoting her time to teaching me the art of cooking, and to my father, Sri Shyam Lal, for his encouragement and appreciation for my cooking.

**Preparation and cooking time**

35 Min.

**Serves**

4-5 Persons

## Ingredients

- 1 cup water chestnut flour
- ½ cup spinach, finely chopped
- 1 tablespoon white sesame seeds
- 1 teaspoon cumin seeds
- 1 teaspoon salt
- ⅛ teaspoon black pepper
- 1 cup (240 ml) water, or as needed
- 2 cups potatoes, peeled and cut into thin slices
- oil for deep-frying

## Procedure

1. Mix the flour, spinach, sesame seeds, cumin seeds, salt, and black pepper in a bowl. Slowly add enough water until a thick batter-like consistency.

2. Heat the oil in a 2½-inch (6.5 cm) deep frying pan until the temperature reaches 300°F (148°C). Dip the potato slices in the batter so they are completely covered. Carefully place the pakoras into the hot oil without crowding them. Fry for 3-4 minutes or until they become golden brown, then turn them over and maintaining a temperature of 300°F (148°C) to 350°F (177°C), and fry for 2-3 minutes more or until they become golden brown.

3. Remove them with a slotted spoon and place them on a paper towel to absorb the extra oil.

# Pumpkin Pakora

**Preparation and cooking time**

25 Min.

**Serves**

3-4 Persons

## Ingredients

- ½ cup buckwheat flour
- ½ cup amaranth flour
- 1 cup pumpkin, peeled, seeded, and cut into ¼-inch (6 mm) pieces
- 1¼ teaspoons salt
- 1 teaspoon cumin powder
- ¼ teaspoon black pepper
- 2 tablespoons cilantro, finely chopped
- ½ cup (120 ml) + 2 tablespoons water, or as needed
- oil for deep-frying

## Procedure

1. Combine the buckwheat flour, amaranth flour, pumpkin, salt, cumin powder, black pepper, and cilantro in a bowl. Mix well. Slowly add enough water and mix well until the consistency is like mashed potatoes.

2. Heat the oil in a 2½-inch (6.5 cm) deep frying pan until the temperature reaches 250°F (121°C). Take a little mixture (about 1 tablespoon) between your fingers and thumb and drop it carefully into the hot oil. Put in as many pakoras as you can without crowing them.

3. Occasionally stirring them, fry for about 10-12 minutes or until golden brown on both sides, maintaining a temperature of 250°F (121°C) to 300°F (148°C).

4. Remove them with a slotted spoon and place them on a paper towel to absorb the extra oil.

# Green Quinoa Pakora

**Preparation and cooking time**

25 Min.

**Serves**

3-4 Persons

## Ingredients

- 2 cups cooked quinoa
- 2 cups spinach
- ¾ tablespoon ginger root peeled and roughly chopped
- ¾ tablespoon green chilies, roughly chopped
- 1 teaspoon salt
- ¾ cup amaranth flour
- oil for deep-frying

## Procedure

1. Combine the quinoa, spinach, ginger root, and green chilies in a blender. Add a little water and blend until it becomes a smooth mixture. Transfer to a bowl.

2. Add the salt and amaranth flour. Mix well.

3. Heat the oil in a 2½-inch (6.5 cm) deep frying pan until the temperature reaches 300°F (148°C). Take about 1 tablespoon of the mixture between your fingers and thumb and drop it carefully into the hot oil without crowding them.

4. Occasionally move the pakoras with a wooden spatula and fry them for about 4-5 minutes or until they are done, maintaining a temperature of 300°F (148°C) to 350°F (177°C).

5. Remove them with a slotted spoon and place them on a paper towel to absorb the extra oil.

# Kachori

His Divine Grace A.C. Bhaktivedanta Swami Prabhupada, Founder-Acarya of the International Society for Krishna Consciousness, was very fond of kachoris and in his youth was lovingly nicknamed "Kachori Mukhi" by his father. At the beginning of the Hare Kṛṣṇa Movement, he would cook the Sunday feasts himself and personally teach his followers how to cook. Srila Prabhupada used all-purpose flour to make kachoris, but I am using non-grain flours here.

**Preparation and cooking time**

35 Min.

**Makes**

4 Kachoris

## Ingredients

***THE DOUGH***

- ¾ cup buckwheat flour
- ¾ cup water chestnut flour
- ¾ teaspoon salt
- 1 tablespoon melted oil
- ½ cup (120 ml) water, or as needed

***THE FILLING***

- 1½ tablespoons oil
- ¼ teaspoon asafetida
- 2½ tablespoons cashews, finely chopped
- 1 tablespoon green chilies, finely chopped
- 1 tablespoon ginger root, peeled and grated
- 1 cup potatoes, boiled, peeled, and mashed
- ½ teaspoon salt
- 1½ tablespoons cilantro, finely chopped
- oil for deep-frying

## Procedure

***THE DOUGH***

Mix the buckwheat flour, water chestnut flour, salt, and oil in a bowl, slowly adding enough water to make a medium-soft dough. Knead for 1-2 minutes and set aside.

***THE FILLING***

1. Heat the oil in a frying pan over medium heat. When it is hot but not smoking, add the asafetida and sauté for a few seconds. Add the cashews, green chilies, and ginger root. Continuously stirring, cook for 1-2 minutes or until the cashews become light brown.

2. Add the potatoes and salt. Continuously stirring, cook for 1-2 minutes. Add the cilantro. Transfer to a bowl. Divide the mixture into 4 portions.

3. Divide the dough into 4 portions and roll them into smooth balls. Flatten into 4-inch (10 cm) rounds between your palms. Place one portion of the filling in the center of the circle, then bring the sides of the circle up and pinch the seams together. Gently flatten the kachoris. Place on a greased tray.

4. Heat the oil in a 2½-inch (6.5 cm) deep frying pan over medium heat until the temperature reaches 300°F (148°C). Slip the kachoris into the oil without crowding them. Slowly fry them for 4-5 minutes or until brown, then carefully turn them over. Fry them for 3-4 minutes more, maintaining a temperature of 300°F (148°C) to 325°F (162°C).

5. Remove them with a slotted spoon and place them on a paper towel to absorb the extra oil.

# Baked Cauliflower Pakora

**Preparation and cooking time**

20 Min.

**Baking Time**

25-30 Min.

**Serves**

4-5 Persons

## Ingredients

- 1 cup quinoa
- 1½ tablespoons green chilies, roughly chopped
- 1½ tablespoons ginger root peeled and finely chopped
- 1⅓ cups (320ml) water, or as needed
- 1½ teaspoons salt
- 1 teaspoon cumin powder
- 1 teaspoon coriander powder
- ⅛ teaspoon black pepper
- 1 tablespoon white sesame seeds
- 3 cups cauliflower, cut into 2-inch (5 cm) florets

## Procedure

1. Combine the quinoa, green chilies, ginger root, and water in a blender. Blend until a smooth and thick batter-like consistency. You can add extra water or quinoa if necessary.

2. Transfer to a bowl. Add the salt, cumin powder, coriander powder, black pepper, and sesame seeds. Mix well.

3. Place parchment (baking) paper onto a baking tray. Brush with oil. Dip the cauliflower florets in the batter so they are completely covered. Shake slightly so any extra batter comes off. Place on the baking tray.

4. Bake the pakoras in a preheated oven at 350°F (177°C) for 25-30 minutes or until they are done.

# Plantain Patties

**Preparation and cooking time**

30 Min.

**Makes**

8 Patties

## Ingredients

- 2 cups plantains, boiled, peeled, and mashed
- ¼ cup amaranth flour
- 1 teaspoon salt
- ⅛ teaspoon cayenne pepper
- 1 teaspoon cumin powder
- 1 teaspoon lemon juice
- 3 tablespoons cilantro, finely chopped
- oil for pan-frying

## Procedure

1. Combine all the ingredients in a bowl. Mix well. Divide the mixture into 8 portions and roll each portion into a ball. If the mixture is too dry, you can add a little water. Gently flatten them into 2-inch (5 cm) patties and place them on a greased tray.

2. Preheat a flat, non-stick griddle. When it reaches medium heat, place ½-1 teaspoon oil in the pan. Place in as many patties as possible without crowding them. After 1-2 minutes, drizzle ⅓ teaspoon oil around the edge of each patty. Cook them for 4-5 minutes more or until golden brown, then carefully turn them over with a spatula. Drizzle ¼ teaspoon oil around the edges of each patty and cook for 3-4 minutes or until golden brown. Repeat the same process until all the patties are cooked.

NOTE: You can cook the patties without using oil.

# Green Cutlet

The vegetables in this recipe must be blended only in a food processor. If you blend the vegetables in a blender, the mixture will be very wet and juicy, which will not work for this preparation.

| Preparation and cooking time | Makes |
|---|---|
| 25 Min. | 8 Cutlets |

## Ingredients

- 2 cups kale
- 1 cup green cabbage, shredded
- 1 cup broccoli, cut into medium sized florets
- ½ cup buckwheat flour
- 1 tablespoon ginger root, peeled and grated
- ½ teaspoon salt
- ¼ teaspoon black pepper
- oil for pan-frying

## Procedure

1. Combine the kale, cabbage, and broccoli in a food processor. Grind until it becomes smooth. Transfer to a bowl.

2. Add the buckwheat flour, ginger root, salt, and black pepper. Mix well. Divide the mixture into 8 portions and roll each portion into a ball. Gently flatten them into 2-inch (5 cm) cutlets and place them on a greased tray.

3. Preheat a flat, non-stick griddle. When it reaches medium heat, place ½-1 teaspoon oil in the pan. Place in as many cutlets as possible without crowding them. After 1-2 minutes, drizzle ⅓ teaspoon oil around the edge of each cutlet. Cook them for 4-5 minutes more or until golden brown, then carefully turn them over with a spatula. Drizzle ¼ teaspoon oil over each cutlet and ½ teaspoon oil around the edges and cook for 4-5 minutes or until golden brown. Repeat the same process until all the cutlets are cooked.

NOTE: You can cook the cutlets without using oil.

# Quinoa And Spinach Cutlet

**Preparation and cooking time**

25 Min.

**Makes**

8 Cutlets

## Ingredients

- 2 cups cooked quinoa
- 1 cup spinach, finely chopped
- ⅓ cup water chestnut flour
- ½ tablespoon green chilies, finely chopped
- ½ tablespoon ginger root, peeled and grated
- 1¼ teaspoons salt
- 1 teaspoon lemon juice
- oil for pan-frying

## Procedure

1. Combine all the ingredients in a bowl. Mix well. Divide the mixture into 8 portions and roll each portion into a ball. Gently flatten them into 2-inch (5 cm) patties and place them on a greased tray.

2. Preheat a flat, non-stick griddle. Place ½-1 teaspoon of oil in the pan when it reaches medium heat. Place in as many cutlets as possible without crowding them. After 1-2 minutes, drizzle 1 teaspoon of oil around the edge of each cutlet. Cook them for a few minutes more or until golden brown, then carefully turn them over with a spatula. Drizzle ¼ teaspoon of oil over each cutlet and ½ teaspoon oil around the edges and cook for 2-3 minutes or until golden brown.

3. Repeat the same process until all the cutlets are cooked.

NOTE: Make sure that there is no moisture in the quinoa; otherwise, the cutlets will be very fragile.

# Namak Para

It is a great blessing to cook new preparations for the pleasure of Their Lordships, Sri Sri Radha Golokananda, who are at New Goloka in North Carolina, US. Devotees like this savory very much.

**Preparation and cooking time**

25 Min.

**Serves**

3-4 Persons

## Ingredients

- ½ cup amaranth flour
- ½ cup water chestnut flour
- 1 tablespoon oil
- ½ teaspoon salt
- 1 tablespoon white sesame seeds
- 1 teaspoon cumin seeds
- ¼ teaspoon peppercorns, freshly and coarsely ground
- ⅓ cup (80 ml) water or as needed oil for deep-frying

## Procedure

1. Combine the flours, oil, salt, sesame seeds, cumin seeds, and peppercorns in a bowl. Mix well. Slowly add enough water to make a firm dough.

2. Divide the dough into 3 portions and roll each portion into a ball. On a greased working surface or between 2 greased zip lock bags, roll each ball into a 5-inch (12.7 cm) round. Place on a greased tray.

3. Prick the rounds 5-6 places with a fork so they do not puff during frying. Cut into your desired shape. Heat the oil in a 2½-inch (6.5 cm) deep frying pan until the temperature reaches 250°F (121°C). Place the namak para in the oil without crowding them and fry for 4-5 minutes on both sides or until they become brown.

4. Remove namak para with a slotted spoon and place them on a paper towel to absorb the extra oil.

# Plum Chutney

Plum chutney is one of Srimati Radharani's favorite dishes. Srimati Radharani is the primeval, internal potency of Lord Kṛṣṇa. She is worshipable by everyone and the greatest devotee of Lord Kṛṣṇa.

**Preparation time**

8 Min.

**Makes**

1½ cups

## Ingredients

- 2 cups plums, seeded and cut into small pieces
- ⅓ cup raisins
- ¼ cup walnuts
- ½ teaspoon salt
- 1 teaspoon cumin seeds
- ½ cup (120 ml) water, or as needed

## Procedure

Place all the ingredients in a blender and process to a smooth paste.

# Hari Chutney

Hari is the Hindi name for the color green. It's also one of the names of Lord Kṛṣṇa, which means one who takes away all miseries.

**Preparation time**

10 Min.

**Makes**

1¼ cups

## Ingredients

- 3 cups fresh mint leaves
- 1/3 cup sunflower seeds
- 1 tablespoon ginger root, peeled and roughly chopped
- 1 tablespoon green chili, roughly chopped
- 1 teaspoon salt
- 1 teaspoon cumin seeds
- ½ cup water, or as needed
- 2 tablespoons lemon juice

## Procedure

Place all the ingredients in a blender and process to a smooth paste.

Cashew and Raisin Chutney

# Cashew And Raisin Chutney

**Preparation and cooking time**

15 Min.

**Makes**

½ cup

## Ingredients

- ½ cup cashew pieces
- 1 tablespoon coconut oil
- 10-12 fresh curry leaves
- ¼ cup raisins
- ¾ tablespoon green chilies, finely chopped
- ⅓ teaspoon salt
- ½ cup (120 ml) water, or as needed

## Procedure

1. Place the cashew pieces in a frying pan. Continuously stirring, dry roast them over medium heat for 1-2 minutes or until they turn light brown. Allow to cool.

2. Heat the oil in a frying pan over medium heat. When it is hot but not smoking, add the curry leaves and cook for a few seconds. Add the raisins. Continuously stirring, cook for 1-2 minutes. Allow to cool. Transfer to a blender.

3. Add the cashew pieces, green chilies, salt, and enough water and process to a smooth paste.

# Apricot Chutney

**Preparation time**

8 Min.

**Makes**

1½ cup

## Ingredients

- 1 cup apricots, dried
- 1 tablespoon ginger root, peeled and roughly chopped
- ½ teaspoon salt
- ¼ teaspoon black pepper
- 2 tablespoons lemon juice
- 1 cup (240 ml) water, or as needed

## Procedure

Place all the ingredients in a blender and process to a smooth paste.

# Coconut And Cranberry Chutney

**Preparation time**

8 Min.

**Makes**

1 cup

## Ingredients

- ½ cup grated, dried coconut
- ½ cup cranberries, dried
- ¾ tablespoons green chilies, roughly chopped
- ½ teaspoon salt
- 1 teaspoon cumin seeds
- ¾ tablespoon lemon juice
- 1 cup (240 ml) water, or as needed

## Procedure

Place all the ingredients in a blender and process to a smooth paste.

# Coconut And Coriander Chutney

**Preparation time**

8 Min.

**Makes**

1 Cup

## Ingredients

- ¼ cup grated, dried, coconut
- 1 cup cilantro
- ⅓ teaspoon salt
- ¾ tablespoon green chilies, roughly chopped
- 1 teaspoon lemon juice
- ½ cup (120 ml) water, or as needed

## Procedure

Place all the ingredients in a blender and process to a smooth paste.

# Peanut Chutney

**Preparation and cooking time**

12 Min.

**Makes**

1 Cup

## Ingredients

- ¾ tablespoon oil
- ¼ teaspoon asafetida
- 10-12 fresh curry leaves
- 1 cup peanuts
- ⅓ teaspoon salt
- ½ tablespoon green chilies, roughly chopped
- ¾ tablespoon lemon juice
- ¾ cup (180 ml) water, or as needed

## Procedure

1. Heat the oil in a frying pan over medium heat. When it is hot but not smoking, add the asafetida and curry leaves. Cook for a few seconds.

2. Add the peanuts. Continuously stirring, cook them for 1-2 minutes or until they turn light brown. Transfer to a bowl and allow to cool.

3. Transfer to a blender. Add all the remaining ingredients and process to a smooth paste.

# Coriander Chutney

**Preparation time**

12 Min.

**Makes**

1 Cup

## Ingredients

- 2 cups cilantro
- ⅓ cup cucumbers peeled and cut into small pieces
- ⅓ cup cashew pieces, unsalted and roasted
- 1 tablespoon green chilies, roughly chopped
- 1 tablespoon lemon juice
- ¾ teaspoon salt
- 1 teaspoon cumin seeds
- ⅓ cup (80 ml) water, or as needed

## Procedure

Place all the ingredients in a blender and process to a smooth paste.

Coriander Chutney

# Pumpkin Chutney

**Preparation and cooking time**

20 Min.

**Makes**

¾ cup

## Ingredients

- ½ tablespoon oil
- ¾ teaspoon cumin seeds
- 1 cup pumpkin, peeled, seeded, and shredded
- ⅓ teaspoon salt
- ⅛ teaspoon cayenne pepper
- ⅓ teaspoon turmeric
- 1 teaspoon coriander powder
- ¾ cup (180 ml) water, or as needed
- 1 tablespoon sugar
- ½ tablespoon lemon juice

## Procedure

1. Heat the oil in a frying pan over medium heat. When it is hot but not smoking, add the cumin seeds and sauté until they turn brown.

2. Add the pumpkin, salt, cayenne pepper, turmeric, coriander powder, and water. Cover and cook over medium heat for 7-8 minutes or until the pumpkin is cooked. While cooking, stir a few times with a wooden spatula to make sure it is evenly cooked and does not stick to the bottom of the pan.

3. Add the sugar and lemon juice. Cook for a few minutes more or until the liquid evaporates.

# Raisin Chutney

**Preparation time**

10 Min.

**Makes**

¾ Cup

## Ingredients

- 1 cup raisins
- 1 tablespoon ginger root, peeled and grated
- ½ teaspoon salt
- ⅛ teaspoon black pepper
- 2 tablespoons lemon or lime juice
- ⅓ cup (80 ml) water, or as needed

## Procedure

Place all the ingredients in a blender and process to a smooth paste.

# Mango And Pineapple Chutney

**Preparation and cooking time**

15 Min.

**Makes**

1 Cup

## Ingredients

- 2 teaspoons oil
- ½ teaspoon cumin seeds
- 1 cup ripe mangos, peeled, seeded, and finely chopped
- 1 cup pineapple, peeled and finely chopped
- ½ teaspoon salt
- ⅛ teaspoon cayenne pepper
- ⅛ teaspoon black pepper
- ¼ teaspoon turmeric
- ½ teaspoon coriander powder
- 2 tablespoons water
- 1½ tablespoons agave nectar or 2 tablespoons sugar

## Procedure

1. Heat the oil in a non-stick frying pan over medium heat. When it is hot but not smoking, add the cumin seeds and sauté until light brown. Add the mango, pineapple, salt, cayenne pepper, black pepper, turmeric, coriander powder, and water. Mix well. Cover and cook on low heat for 7-8 minutes or until the fruits are very soft.

2. Uncover the pan and stir a few times with a wooden spatula to make sure the fruits are evenly cooked and do not stick. You can add extra water if needed. Then, add the agave nectar or sugar. Mix well.

# Desserts and Beverages

ॐ

# Deserts and Beverages

# Sankirtan Sweet

The ISKCON movement is known as the sankirtan movement. Those who have devoted their lives to this movement distribute the mercy of Lord Kṛṣṇa by distributing spiritual books, the holy name, and prasada (sacred food). This grain, gluten, sugar, and dairy-free recipe will satisfy everyone, whether or not they are on a special diet.

Preparation and cooking time
**20 Min.**

Makes
**12 Pieces**

## Ingredients

- 2 tablespoons coconut oil
- ½ cup blanched peanuts, ground
- ½ cup cashews, ground
- ½ cup walnuts, ground
- ¾ cup dates, pitted and ground
- ¾ cup dried apricots, ground
- 3 tablespoons orange juice

## Procedure

1. Heat the oil in a frying pan. Add the peanuts, cashews, and walnuts. Continuously stirring on medium heat, cook the nuts for 3-4 minutes or until they become light brown.

2. Turn off the heat. Add the dates and apricots and mix well.

3. Transfer to a bowl. Allow to cool. Add the orange juice and mix well.

4. Divide the mixture into 12 portions. Roll into balls.

# Carrot Halva

College students in the USA are very fond of halva, so I am adding several halva recipes in my cookbook just for them!

Preparation and cooking time
**25 Min.**

Serves
**3-4 Persons**

## Ingredients

- 3 cups carrots, peeled and cut into 1-inch (2.5 cm) pieces
- ½ cup coconut oil
- ⅓ cup sugar
- ⅓ cup cashews, roasted and finely chopped

## Procedure

1. Blend the carrots in a food processor until smooth, adding water as needed.

2. Heat the oil in a frying pan and add the ground carrots. Continuously stirring, cook over medium-high heat for about 10-12 minutes.

3. Add the sugar and continuously stirring, cook for about 3-4 minutes more or until thick. Add the cashews and mix well.

# Potato Halva

Preparation and cooking time
**25 Min.**

Serves
**2-3 Persons**

## Ingredients

- ¼ cup cashew butter
- ½ cup coconut oil
- 2 cups potatoes, boiled, peeled, and mashed
- ½ cup sugar
- 2 tablespoons pistachios, finely chopped

## Procedure

1. Melt the cashew butter and coconut oil in a frying pan over medium heat and add the mashed potatoes. Continuously stirring, cook for about 8-10 minutes.

2. Add the sugar and continuously stirring, cook for about 3-4 minutes more or until thick. Transfer to a bowl. Garnish with pistachios.

# Pumpkin Halva

Preparation and cooking time
**35 Min.**

Serves
**3-4 Persons**

## Ingredients

- 4 cups pumpkin, peeled, seeded, and roughly chopped
- ¾ cup coconut oil
- ¼ cup cashews, finely chopped
- ½ cup sugar
- ½ teaspoon cardamom powder

## Procedure

1. Blend the pumpkin in a blender until smooth. Add a little water if required.

2. Heat the oil in a frying pan and add the cashews. Continuously stirring, cook over medium heat for 1-2 minutes or until light brown.

3. Add the pumpkin. Continuously stirring, cook for about 15-20 minutes over medium-high heat or until it is cooked. Add the sugar and cardamom powder. Continuously stirring, cook for about 3-4 minutes more or until the halva is thick.

# Plantain Halva

Preparation and cooking time
**25 Min.**

Serves
**4-5 Persons**

## Ingredients

- ¾ cup coconut oil
- 2 tablespoons cashews, finely chopped
- 2 tablespoons almonds, finely chopped
- 2 cups plantains, boiled, peeled, and mashed
- 1 cup coconut milk
- ¾ cup sugar
- ½ teaspoon cardamom powder
- 2 tablespoons finely chopped pistachios for garnish

## Procedure

1. Heat the oil in a non-stick frying pan. Add the cashews and almonds and continuously stirring, cook over medium heat for about 2-3 minutes, or until the nuts become light brown.

2. Add the plantains and continuously stirring, cook over medium heat for about 5-7 minutes, or until the plantain is cooked.

3. Add the coconut milk and continuously stirring, cook over medium heat for about 5-7 minutes or until the halva thickens.

4. Add the sugar and cardamom. Continuously stirring, cook for 2-3 minutes or until the desired consistency. Transfer to a bowl. Garnish with pistachios.

NOTE: You can increase or decrease the quantity of coconut oil and sugar according to your taste.

# Quinoa Halva

Preparation and cooking time
**20 Min.**

Serves
**4-5 Persons**

## Ingredients

- 1 cup sugar
- 2 cups (480 ml) water
- ¾ cup coconut oil
- ¼ cup walnuts, roughly chopped
- 1 cup quinoa flour

## Procedure

1. Place the sugar and water in a 2-quart saucepan and boil over medium heat until the sugar dissolves. Cover and on the lowest heat, allow the water to continue boiling.

2. Heat the oil in a frying pan. Add the walnuts and continuously stirring, cook over medium heat for about 2-3 minutes or until the walnuts become light brown.

3. Add the flour and continuously stirring, cook over medium heat for about 4-5 minutes, or until the flour is light brown. Turn the heat off, and slowly pour the sugar water into the flour and stir. The mixture will sputter but will absorb the water quickly. Stir the halva until it becomes thick.

NOTE: You can buy quinoa flour from the health food store, or you can grind quinoa in a blender to make the flour.

# Apple Halva

Preparation and cooking time
**25 Min.**

Serves
**2-3 Persons**

## Ingredients

- 3 tablespoons coconut oil
- ⅓ cup walnuts, finely chopped
- ⅓ cup dates, pitted and finely chopped
- 2 cups apples, peeled, cored, and grated
- 2½ tablespoons sugar
- ½ teaspoon cardamom powder
- 2 tablespoons sliced almonds for garnish

## Procedure

1. Heat the oil in a frying pan. Add the walnuts and dates. Continuously stirring, cook for 2-3 minutes over medium heat or until they are done.

2. Add the apples. Frequently stirring, cook for 5-7 minutes over medium heat or until it is done.

3. Add the sugar and cardamom powder. Cook for 1-2 minutes more.

4. Transfer to a bowl. Garnish with almonds.

# Sweet Quinoa

Preparation and cooking time
**25 Min.**

Serves
**3-4 Persons**

## Ingredients

- 1½ tablespoons coconut oil
- ¼ cup sliced almonds
- ½ cup (120 ml) water
- ½ cup blueberries
- ½ cup sugar
- 1 cup cooked quinoa

## Procedure

1. Heat the oil in a 3-quart saucepan. Add the sliced almonds. Continuously stirring, cook over medium heat for 1-2 minutes or until they turn brown.

2. Add the water and allow it to boil. Add the blueberries. Cover the pan and cook over medium heat for 2-3 minutes or until the blueberries are soft. Add the sugar and allow it to dissolve.

3. Add the quinoa. Cook for 1-2 minutes more or until the liquid evaporates.

# Laddu

Lord Kṛṣṇa is also known as 'Laddu Gopal' because He is very fond of laddus. Once, I made grain-free laddus for His pleasure, and the devotees in New Goloka liked them very much.

Preparation and cooking time
**25 Min.**

Makes
**20 Laddus**

## Ingredients

- 1½ cups coconut oil
- 1 cup almonds, finely ground
- 2 cups amaranth flour
- 1 cup grated, dried coconut
- ¾ teaspoon cardamom powder
- 2 cups powdered sugar

## Procedure

1. Heat the oil in a 6-quart stockpot and add the almonds. Continuously stirring, cook over medium heat for about 2-3 minutes or until they turn light brown.

2. Add the flour. Continuously stirring, cook over medium heat for about 7-8 minutes or until it becomes light brown.

3. Transfer to a bowl. Add the coconut, cardamom, and sugar. Mix well. Allow to cool.

4. Divide the mixture into 20 portions and roll them into medium-sized balls.

NOTE: If the mixture is too soft to roll, place it in the refrigerator for a while.

# Coconut Laddu

I also like to listen to my spiritual master's kirtans and lectures while cooking, which helps me focus and keep my connection with him, who is the source of all my devotional services.

Preparation and cooking time
**30 Min.**

Makes
**6 Laddus**

## Ingredients

- 2 cups coconut milk
- 1½ cups grated, dried coconut
- ¾ cup sugar
- ¼ cup grated, dried coconut for garnish

## Procedure

1. Combine the coconut milk, grated coconut, and sugar in a blender. Blend to a smooth paste. Transfer the paste to a 6-quart stockpot. Continuously stirring, cook on medium heat for 12-15 minutes or until the mixture thickens.

2. Transfer to a bowl and allow the mixture to cool. Divide the mixture into 6 portions and roll them into medium-sized balls, then roll them into the grated coconut. You may grease your palms so you can roll the laddus easily.

# Sweet Pakora

Preparation and cooking time
**20 Min.**

Serves
**3-4 Persons**

## Ingredients

- 1 cup water chestnut flour
- ¾ cup ripe bananas, peeled and mashed
- 2 tablespoons sugar
- pinch of baking soda
- 3 tablespoons water, or as needed
- 2 tablespoons powdered sugar
- oil for deep-frying

## Procedure

1. Combine the flour, bananas, sugar, and baking soda in a bowl. Slowly add enough water and whisk to make the consistency like mashed potatoes.

2. Heat the oil in a 2½-inch (6.5 cm) deep frying pan until the temperature reaches 300°F (148°C). Take about 1 tablespoon of the mixture between your fingers and thumb and carefully place it into the hot oil without crowding the pieces. Occasionally move the pakoras with a spatula and fry until golden brown, maintaining a temperature of 300°F (148°C) to 325°F (162°C).

3. Remove them with a slotted spoon. Place them in a bowl. When they are not too hot but still warm, add powdered sugar. Mix gently.

# Nimai Cookies

Nimai is one of the childhood names of Lord Caitanya, and He is called this because He appeared under a neem tree. So this recipe is dedicated to Him, whose childhood pastimes are very pleasing to His devotees.

Baking Time **10-12 Min.**

Preparation and cooking time **5 Min.**

Makes **8 Cookies**

## Ingredients

- 1 cup cashew pieces
- ¾ cup raisins
- 3 tablespoons tahini
- ¼ cup grated, dried coconut

## Procedure

1. Combine the cashew pieces, raisins, and tahini in a food processor and process to a smooth mixture. Transfer to a bowl.

2. Divide the mixture into 8 portions and roll each portion into a ball, then flatten them into cookies and roll them in the grated coconut. Place on a greased 9 x 13-inch (22.5 x 32.5 cm) baking tray.

3. Bake the cookies in a preheated oven at 350°F (177°C) for 10-12 minutes or until light brown, then allow them to cool. Carefully remove the cookies from the baking tray with a knife or metal spatula.

# Cake

Baking Time
**30-35 Min.**

Preparation time
**15 Min.**

Makes
**One 9" Round Cake**

## Ingredients

- 1 cup unsweetened almond milk (page 149)
- ½ cup sunflower oil
- 1 tablespoon lemon juice
- 1 tablespoon flavoring of your choice
- 1 cup sugar
- ½ teaspoon salt
- 1 teaspoon baking soda
- 1½ cups water chestnut flour

***THE FROSTING***

- ¾ cup powdered sugar
- 1½ tablespoons lemon juice
- ½ cup nuts of your choice, finely chopped

## Procedure

1. Combine the almond milk, oil, lemon juice, flavoring, sugar, salt, and baking soda in a bowl. Mix well.

2. Add the flour. Mix well, making sure there are no lumps. You can add little extra flour or water if needed.

3. Grease the bottom and sides of a 9-inch round cake pan with oil. Sprinkle a little dry flour in the pan. Shake around until the pan is lightly coated. Pour the batter into the prepared pan. Gently tap the pan on the counter to remove air bubbles before putting it in the oven.

4. Bake the cake in a preheated oven at 325°F (162°C) for 30-35 minutes or until the top part of the cake is brown and does not stick to a knife when inserted. Allow to cool.

***THE FROSTING***

Place the powdered sugar and lemon juice in a bowl. Mix well. Drizzle it on the top of the cake with a spoon. Sprinkle the nuts over it. Cut into the desired shape.

NOTE: If the cake is too soft to cut, you may place it in the freezer for a few minutes.

# Muffins

Baking Time
**25-30 Min.**

Preparation time
**15 Min.**

Makes
**12-16 Muffins**

## Ingredients

- 1 cup unsweetened almond milk (page 149)
- ½ cup sunflower oil
- 1 tablespoon lemon juice
- 1 cup ripe bananas, peeled and mashed
- ¾ cup sugar
- ½ teaspoon salt
- 1 teaspoon baking soda
- 2 cups buckwheat flour
- ½ cup nuts of your choice, finely chopped

## Procedure

1. Combine the almond milk, oil, lemon juice, bananas, sugar, salt, and baking soda in a bowl. Mix Well.

2. Add the flour and mix well. Add the nuts. Mix gently.

3. Place baking cups in a muffin pan. Spoon the batter into the cups till 2/3 full. Bake in a preheated oven at 325°F (162°C) for 25-30 minutes or until the muffins turn brown.

NOTE: You may spread any type of fruit jam on the top of the muffins after they are baked and cooled.

# Fruit Pudding

Preparation time
**5 Min.**

Serves
**2-3 Persons**

## Ingredients

- 3 cups mixed frozen fruits
- 1 cup coconut milk
- 1½ tablespoons agave nectar or 2 tablespoons sugar

## Procedure

Place all the ingredients in a blender and process until the desired consistency.

# Unsweetened Almond Milk

I am adding this recipe because I use unsweetened almond milk in a few recipes. If making a drink, you can add a sweetener of your choice.

Almond Soaking Time **6-8 Hours**

Preparation time **10 Min.**

Makes **2 Cups**

## Ingredients

- 1 cup whole almonds
- 5 cups (1200 ml) water

## Procedure

1. Soak the almonds in 2 cups (480 ml) of water for 6-8 hours, then strain and rinse the almonds thoroughly.

2. Combine the soaked almonds and the remaining 3 cups (720 ml) of water in a blender. Process on high speed until creamy and smooth.

3. Strain through a muslin-lined strainer and using a spoon, press the pulp to extract as much milk as possible.

# Priya Nectar

Soaking Time
**2 Hours**

Preparation time
**10 Min.**

Serves
**2 Persons**

## Ingredients

- 2 cups unsweetened almond milk (page 149)
- 1½ tablespoons white poppy seeds
- 1 tablespoon pistachios, roughly chopped
- ½ teaspoon cardamom seeds
- 4-5 threads of saffron
- 3 tablespoons sugar
- 1 teaspoon rosewater
- ½ cup ice cubes

## Procedure

1. Combine the almond milk, poppy seeds, pistachios, cardamom seeds, and saffron in a bowl. Place in the refrigerator for 2 hours.

2. Transfer to a blender. Add the sugar, rosewater, and ice cubes and blend until smooth.

# Lime And Mint Nectar

Preparation time
**10 Min.**

Serves
**2-3 Persons**

## Ingredients

- 1 medium-sized lime, seeded and cut into small pieces with skin
- 12-15 fresh mint leaves
- 2½ cups (600 ml) water
- 4 tablespoons sugar
- ½ cup ice cubes

## Procedure

Place all the ingredients in a blender and process to a smooth puree. Strain through a muslin-lined strainer.

# Green Nectar

Preparation time
**8 Min.**

Serves
**3-4 Persons**

## Ingredients

- 3 cups coconut water
- 1 cup kale or spinach
- 1 cup frozen pineapple chunks
- 1 cup frozen mango chunks
- ½ cup ice cubes

## Procedure

Place all the ingredients in a blender and process to a smooth puree.

# Mango Lassi

Preparation time
**8 Min.**

Serves
**2-3 Persons**

## Ingredients

- 2 cups coconut milk
- 1 cup ripe mango, peeled, seeded and cut into small pieces
- 2½ tablespoons sugar
- 2 cups ice cubes, or as needed

## Procedure

Place all the ingredients in a blender and process to a smooth puree.

# Watermelon Lemonade

Preparation time
**8 Min.**

Serves
**2-3 Persons**

## Ingredients

- 4 cups watermelon, peeled, seeded, and cut into pieces
- 2 tablespoons lemon juice
- 3 tablespoons sugar
- ½ cup ice cubes

## Procedure

Place all the ingredients in a blender and process to a smooth puree.

# Pineapple And Pistachio Shake

Pistachio soaking time
**15-20 Min.**

Preparation time
**15 Min.**

Serves
**1-2 Persons**

## Ingredients

- 12-15 pistachios
- ½ cup (120 ml) boiling water
- 2 cups unsweetened almond milk (page 149)
- 1 cup pineapple, peeled and roughly chopped
- 1½ tablespoons agave nectar or 2 tablespoons sugar
- ½ cup ice cubes

## Procedure

1. Soak the pistachios in boiling water in a covered container for 15-20 minutes, then rinse under cold water. Transfer to a blender.

2. Add the remaining ingredients. Blend until smooth.

# Apple Shake

Preparation time
**7 Min.**

Serves
**1 Person**

## Ingredients

- 1 cup unsweetened almond milk (page 149)
- ½ cup apples, peeled, cored, and cut into small pieces
- ¾ tablespoon agave nectar or 1 tablespoon sugar
- ⅛ teaspoon cinnamon powder
- ½ cup ice cubes

## Procedure

Place all the ingredients in a blender and process to a smooth puree.

# Fruit Smoothie

Preparation time
**10 Min.**

Serves
**2-3 Persons**

## Ingredients

- 1 cup mangoes, peeled, seeded, and cut into small pieces
- 1 cup bananas, peeled and cut into small pieces
- 1 cup strawberries
- 5-6 dates, pitted
- 3 cups (720 ml) cold water
- 1 cup ice cubes

## Procedure

Place all the ingredients in a blender and process to a smooth puree.

# Cashew Milk

Cashew Soaking Time **2-3 Hours**

Preparation time **10 Min.**

Serves **3-4 Persons**

## Ingredients

- 1 cup cashew pieces
- 7 cups (1680 ml) water
- 4-5 dates, pitted
- ¾ tablespoon agave nectar or 1 tablespoon sugar

## Procedure

1. Place the cashew pieces and 3 cups (720 ml) of water in a bowl. Place in the refrigerator for 2-3 hours. Drain the soaked cashew pieces and rinse thoroughly.

2. Transfer to a blender and add the remaining 4 cups (960 ml) of water, the dates, agave nectar, or sugar. Begin with the blender at the lowest setting and gradually work up to the highest setting. Blend until smooth.

# The Author

Krishna Priya Dasi is a disciple of His Holiness Lokanath Swami, a direct disciple of His Divine Grace A.C. Bhaktivedanta Swami Prabhupada, the founder acharya of the International Society for Krishna Consciousness (ISKCON).

Srila Prabhupada is the world's foremost Vedic scholar and teacher, and has authored more than 60 transcendental literatures like *Bhagavad-gita As It Is, Srimad Bhagavatam, Sri Caitanya-Caritamrta*, etc.

Krishna Priya Dasi was born in Rajasthan, India, and raised in Jaipur, the capital of Rajasthan, which is famous for the Sri Sri Radha-Govinda Dev Ji temple and a wide variety of artistic works and activities.
After moving to the New Goloka Temple in North Carolina, USA, in 1996 and marrying Gopal Das, Krishna Priya Dasi started to cook for the Deities, Sri Sri Radha Golokananda. She was desirous of sharing her recipes with others and was inspired to compile *The Art of Indian Sweets, Devotional Dishes, New Goloka Cuisine, and Govinda's Cuisine.* She has also composed devotional poetry books:

*Lotus Lyrics*, a book inspired by His Divine Grace A.C. Bhaktivedanta Swami Prabhupada's *Bhagavad-gita As It Is.*

*Jaya Srila Prabhupada*, a book of 108 verses based on Srila Prabhupada's transcendental teachings.

*Srila Lokanath Swami-The Walking Warrior*, a book of 71 poems glorifying her spiritual master.

Krishna Priya Dasi is also known for her Rajasthani artwork. One of her paintings, Rasa Lila, is featured on the front cover of *Dance of Divine Love* by Graham M. Schweig.

# Glossary

Lord Kṛṣṇa:The Supreme Personality of Godhead.

Srimati Radharani: The eternal consort of Lord Kṛṣṇa.

Lord Balarama: Lord Kṛṣṇa's elder brother and His first expansion. He is the source of all spiritual strength.

Lord Narasimha Dev: The half-lion and half-man incarnation of the Supreme Lord Kṛṣṇa. He is the destroyer of all obstacles on the path of bhakti and is very merciful and protective of all His devotees.

Lord Jagannatha: The Lord of the universe who appeared with His brother Baladeva and sister Subhadra. Their original temple is in Puri in the province of Orissa.

The Pancha-Tattva: A five-fold manifestation of the Supreme Personality of Godhead, Kṛṣṇa, featured as five tattvas (truths), namely, isha-tattva (the Supreme Lord), His expansion tattva, His incarnation tattva, His energy tattva, and His devotee tattva.

Caitanya Mahaprabhu: The Supreme Personality of Godhead, Sri Kṛṣṇa himself, who appeared in the role of a devotee to spread Kṛṣṇa consciousness.

Lord Nityananda: Lord Balarama's expansion who appeared as Lord Caitanya's principal associate and who spread the chanting of the holy names of Lord Kṛṣṇa.

Govardhana Sila: A sacred stone from Govardhan hill in Vrindavan who is non-different than Lord Kṛṣṇa.

Tulasi devi: It's a sacred plant whose leaves are placed on Lord Kṛṣṇa's lotus feet, as well as on all food offerings.

Asta Sakhis: Eight principle gopis of Vrindavan, headed by Lalita and Visakha.

Sad Goswami: The Six Goswamis were the leading disciples of Sri Caitanya Mahaprabhu, headed by Srila Rupa Goswami. They were a group of scholarly and ascetic devotees of Lord Kṛṣṇa, who uncovered many of the hidden places of Lord Kṛṣṇa's pastimes in Vrindavan, and who established temples there.

ISKCON: The International Society for Krishna Consciousness.

Srila Prabhupada: His Divine Grace A.C. Bhaktivedanta Swami Prabhupada, Founder-Acarya of the International Society for Krishna Consciousness.

Acarya: A representative of Lord Kṛṣṇa who teaches by example, a bona fide spiritual master.

Hare Kṛṣṇa or Maha Mantra: The great mantra for deliverance in this age of Kali: Hare Kṛṣṇa, Hare Kṛṣṇa, Kṛṣṇa Kṛṣṇa, Hare Hare/ Hare Rama, Hare Rama, Rama Rama, Hare Hare.

Japa: Meditative chanting of the Hare Kṛṣṇa maha-mantra on beads.

Sankirtan: Congregational chanting of the Hare Kṛṣṇa maha-mantra.

Bhagavad-gita: The sacred book in which Lord Kṛṣṇa gives the essence of knowledge to His friend and disciple, Arjuna.

Srimad Bhagavatam: Lord Kṛṣṇa's literary incarnation, which has eighteen thousand verses and is considered the topmost Vedic literature.

Sri Caitanya-caritamrta: The life and teachings of Sri Caitanya Mahaprabhu, the Golden Avatar. It was originally written in Bengali and has been translated into English by His Divine Grace A.C. Bhaktivedanta Swami Prabhupada,

Vrindavan: The transcendental and eternal abode of Lord Kṛṣṇa, mirrored on earth as the town in north India where 5,000 years ago, Lord Kṛṣṇa performed His divine pastimes.

Mayapur: Lord Caitanya's birthplace, non-different than Vrindavan, which is situated in West Bengal.

Vaisnava: One who dedicates his life to serving the Supreme Personality of Godhead, 'Kṛṣṇa.'

Bhakti-yoga: Bhakti means 'devotion' and yoga means 'to connect.' Therefore, it means reestablishing our loving relationship with Lord Kṛṣṇa through devotional service.

Karma: The law of action and reaction, "what goes around comes around."

Bhoga: The offering of food to the Supreme Lord, Kṛṣṇa.

Prasada or prasadam: The pure, spiritual, and karma-free food that's been offered in love and devotion for the pleasure of Lord Kṛṣṇa.

Ekadasi: Fasting from grains and beans on the 11th day after the new (waxing) moon and on the 11th day after the full (waning) moon, meant to increase one's devotion to Lord Kṛṣṇa.

Asafetida: A spice also known as hing. Although usually mixed with grains, it can often be found without grains in some ISKCON gift and Indian grocery stores; or you can buy the whole asafetida chunks from Indian grocery stores or purchase it online and then grind it in a spice grinder.

Amaranth flour: Rajagara ka atta, available at health food and Indian grocery stores.

Bell pepper: Capsicum or shimla mirch.

Buckwheat flour: Kuttu ka atta or fanfar ka atta, not a grain, available at health food stores and Indian grocery stores.

Eggplant: Brinjal or baingan.

Peanuts: Ground nut or mungphali.

Okra: Lady fingers or bhindi.

Quinoa: Grain-free seed, very high in protein. It is found in health food stores, most supermarkets, and online.

Sesame seeds: Til, not considered a grain, available at health food and Indian grocery stores.

Tahini: A paste made from sesame seeds, available at health food stores.

Water chestnut flour: Singoda ka atta, available at health food and Indian grocery stores.

# Index